The Math of Christ

The Science of Math Reveals Bible Truths

Other books by the Author
At Ease in the White House
How to Do Business with the Federal Government

Co-Authored With Linda Bauer
Recipes from Historic New England
Recipes from Historic California
Recipes from Historic Colorado
Recipes from Historic America
Recipes from Historic Louisiana
Recipes from Historic Texas

THE MATH OF CHRIST
© 2010 by Col. Stephen M. Bauer

Printed in the United States of America

Published by
Defender Publishing
P.O. Box 5 • Crane, MO 65633
Email: info@defenderpublishing.com

ISBN 098362168-3

The Math of Christ

The Science of Math Reveals Bible Truths

COL. STEPHEN M. BAUER

About the Author

Steve Bauer was "born again" more than fourteen years ago. He is a retired Army Colonel. During his 28 years of service he was an Infantry Officer in Vietnam and on the DMZ in Korea before being selected to serve as a military aide to five presidents. Col Bauer served longer as a White House Military Social Aide than anyone in history. Based on his extensive military career, Steve wrote the books, *At Ease in the White House* and *How to Do Business with the Federal Government*. He is a Distinguished Military Graduate of the ROTC program at Texas A&M, and he has an MBA from George Washington University. Steve's awards include the Presidential Service Badge, Combat Infantryman's Badge, Parachute Badge, Defense Distinguished Service Medal, Legion of Merit, Bronze Star, three Defense Meritorious Service Medals, Army Meritorious Service Medal, and two Army Commendation Medals, among others. Col. Bauer has lectured about social life in the White House for over 22 years on land and on more than 75 cruises.

Steve and his wife Linda have traveled to over 100 countries experiencing and enjoying a wide variety of cultures and cuisines throughout the world, which led to their passion for ethnic and regional foods as well as historic properties. Their cookbook series to date includes Texas, Louisiana, California, Colorado, America, and New England. Linda was elected to the Texas State Board of Education in 2002, and wrote a handbook on homeschooling.

Contact: bauerbooks@gmail.com

Contents

For my wife, Linda,
and our boys, Michael and Christopher,
who worked very hard to bring me to Christ.

Preface

D O YOU BELIEVE THERE IS A HEAVEN? If so, do you believe in Hell? It would be somewhat awkward to imagine that there was one but not the other. If they exist, then they must have been created. There is nothing expounded in the "big bang" theory that suggests that when the world was created, a Heaven and Hell was also created. If they exist at all, it had to have been the work of some supreme being.

Do you believe there is a god? Or even gods? The most popular god is the God of Abraham, Isaac, and Jacob, who also happens to be the God of all Christians and Jews. Many other people happen to reject this particular god, while embracing the notion that there is some god out there running the universe.

That raises the question: If there is some other god in charge, what has he done to reveal himself? If this other god created both a heaven and hell, as well as the universe, why did he fail to tell the people in the world he is credited by some to have created about his marvelous deeds? Why hasn't he left some kind of message for all of mankind to understand how omnipotent he is? The answer to all these questions is apparent. He did none of these things simply because this other god does not exist.

However, the God of Abraham, Isaac, and Jacob did leave

a record of His actions. He did say what He has created, how He did it, and why He did it. The record is commonly known as the Bible. It is the only record among the many dozens of major religions of the world that makes a claim of creation, not only of the world but also of Heaven above and Hell below.

All references made to Heaven and Hell in both historical and modern literature come directly from the Bible. Ironically, some other religions actually use the notion of Heaven and Hell in their descriptions of the afterlife their supporters can achieve, assuming they follow the direction of that faith to get there. But the notion of how Heaven and Hell came into existence is borrowed from the God of Abraham, Isaac, and Jacob.

The Christian God offers it all in one neat package: creation of the universe, including Heaven and Hell; why it was done; and what it takes to participate in this grand plan with the ultimate goal of spending eternity in Heaven with God Himself. The alternative described is spending eternity in Hell. You may decide it is a choice you need not make because you do not believe in Heaven and Hell in the first instance, but that is an unnecessary risk to take. For a better understanding of why you should seriously consider these alternatives, you need to know more about what this omnipotent God says to man: How He has offered man a glimpse of what will happen in the future, how He has detailed events to come centuries before they occurred, and how He has authenticated His message to insure that mankind can accept what He says as the ultimate truth.

Introduction

D O YOU QUESTION HOW A BIBLE COULD BE WRITTEN BY FORTY HUMAN AUTHORS WHO LIVED HUNDREDS OF YEARS APART AND ALSO BE A MESSAGE FROM GOD HIMSELF? Do you wonder why God doesn't come today and update His message, since it was written two thousand years ago? Is it necessary for man to rewrite this ancient text with some modern interpretation that differs significantly from the original just to make it more believable or acceptable to current society? Are you suspicious that someone in history has possibly perpetrated the most massive hoax on man ever devised?

Faithful Christians come to believe in Jesus Christ as the Son of God in many different ways. Ultimately, they all share the fundamental conviction that Christ was in fact sent to Earth to die for their sins, and faith in Him will allow them to spend eternity in Heaven with God the Father and His Son, the Messiah. This certainty is an amazing comfort to many millions who believe in Him, and it is all based on their individual level of faith that He exists and He wants them to spend eternity with Him in Heaven.

Strong, solid faith is sometimes arrived at by simply hearing someone speak of God and Christ as His Son, come to Earth to offer salvation for all mankind. In fact, most people in the world draw their religious beliefs directly from their more senior family members. As a general rule they believe them and trust them to teach them the truth.

Strangers also offer strong and convincing spiritual guidance. Many religious speakers, both Christian and otherwise, can be very convincing when offering a message of salvation or eternal life and many in their audience will accept these statements as a way to get into Heaven for eternity.

Others are moved to accept Jesus as the Son of God after reading about various events in the Bible. Descriptions of how the world was created and advanced into today's environment are powerful arguments that help convince believers that the message offered by the Bible is real and can be relied upon to show them the way to get to Heaven and to spend eternity with God.

This fundamental faith transcends all other beliefs and interpretations of Christian doctrine, but what if you don't yet have that absolute faith in Christ? What if you doubt the authenticity of some human messenger telling you about God's Word? Do they really mean exactly what they are saying? Does this messenger perhaps remind you of someone who would sell you something just for his own benefit and not yours? You know instinctively that a few salesmen are like that, so you would often like to have some additional confirmation of what they are telling you. The sale will be made only when you are convinced.

What if you believe that those who do have resolute faith in Christ and the Bible are merely fantasizing about a world they wished existed, but you simply don't buy it? Are you convinced there is no god at all? Or do you believe it is possible that there is a god of some kind, but it is not the one in the Bible?

What if you think it might be possible that Jesus Christ is the Messiah, but you aren't absolutely sure? Perhaps someone has told you there will be a Messiah someday, but Christ isn't that man. You have a variety of doubts that need to be addressed. Your faith is somewhat weak and uncertain, and you are searching for something more convincing than what a minister, preacher, parent, trusted friend, or stranger knocking at your door has told you. Are these reasons to completely reject and discard the notion of a Savior for all mankind?

Have you studied evolution and become convinced that life began when a microorganism crawled out of a swamp somewhere and eventually became mankind? You believe the story in the Bible about an omnipotent God creating the earth in six days is just a fairy tale? You think it could not have possibly happened that way just because Charles Darwin offered a more believable or modern version of the origin of man?

Are you just so smart, so well educated and intelligent, that you are sure there is no God? You have evaluated all the available evidence, come to your conclusions, and you think everyone who believes in Christ is misguided and wrong? The simple act of comparing various passages in modern Bibles shows that they don't exactly agree and this has convinced you that there are blatant errors in the Scripture.

This apparent disparity gives you a simple, straightforward justification for completely rejecting the message of salvation in God's Word.

Of course, it is entirely possible that you might be right, and all those foolish Christian believers are wasting their time participating in rituals that have no real meaning other than to mollify them while they are here on Earth. They might be just clinging to religion as a way to distract themselves from the possibility of the alternative. To your way of thinking, Karl Marx may have been absolutely correct when he said "religion is the opiate of the masses."

But what do you do if the science of mathematics can show that believers in Christ as the Messiah are right and you are wrong? How do you reconcile the logic of numbers that can show the faith of steadfast Christians has led them to a valid belief while your own perception that they must be dreaming is probably in error?

Why not apply the laws of mathematics to the question and see if it can shed light on the issue and confirm or refute your beliefs? If you are right, you have nothing to lose and it will only strengthen your beliefs. If you are wrong, you have everything to gain by understanding your error, including the opportunity to be absolutely certain of spending eternity with the creator of the universe. That certainty should be worth at least a few minutes of your life.

Everyday Science and Math

SCIENCE HAS DONE MARVELOUS THINGS FOR MANKIND. Our lives are greatly improved by advances brought about by scientific research and discovery. For the past century, man's knowledge has been doubling approximately every two and a half years. Medicine, manufacturing, agriculture, engineering, space exploration, communication technology, and construction, to name only a few areas, are all greatly enhanced by raw science, with the benefits adding immeasurably to the quality of life for the entire human race.

Discoveries by modern scientists not only benefit those in the developed world who can afford to buy new products and services, but through the generosity of wealthy nations, even third world countries can enjoy new medical and scientific advancements. Ironically, studies of ancient practices by tribal witch doctors employed in very primitive third world environments can sometimes also produce startling medical advancements for the modern world. Some cancer researchers are actively exploring the deepest rain forests looking for medicinal cures for cancer as well as other diseases. Tribal witch doctors are sometimes consulted for knowledge of their ancient remedies which leads to modern

COL. STEPHEN M. BAUER

research involving techniques used for many generations in the wildest and most primitive jungle settings.

Just recently scientists discovered that an armored fish, *polypterus senegalus,* has been reported to have survived for millions of years because of the toughness of its scaly covering. Scientists are looking into the possibility that studying this fish may produce better armor protection for our military.

Science is forever moving forward to the advantage of mankind. Christians who believe the Earth was created in six days and has existed for perhaps only six thousand years would not agree with the age of this fish, but that does not prevent science from research that may advance the tools mankind uses to improve life here on Earth.

Mathematics has always been a critical component of all scientific activity. Every airplane built today has been designed and constructed after countless mathematical calculations concerning engine power, lift capabilities, structural strength, flight endurance, and interior design. The distance the aircraft can travel at various altitudes is also calculated by evaluating the total weight of the aircraft plus the weight of the fuel needed to reach a particular destination.

Other math computations include the functionality of the cockpit for the pilots, the design of the galley for the air crew, and the arrangement of the cabin for the safety of the passengers, with the economics of carrying as many passengers as possible trumping comfort. (If you have not noticed that, then you either always fly first class or not at all). Of course, the mathematical computations are actually done by computers at a blinding rate of many millions of calculations every second, but they are purely mathematical in nature.

One obvious example: Science continues to work on the ongoing problem of fuel efficiency, not only for airliners, but realistically for every type of engine imaginable. The various power plants for automobiles and trucks gets most of the attention today, due to the high cost of their fuel, but every form of energy consumption is being studied closely by scientists and inventors alike to figure out how to do more for less. All these calculations of mechanical improvements as well as dollar savings are done using mathematics.

Some people are able to do math quite easily in their heads, while others use calculators, but the end result is the same (if they have done it correctly). They use numbers to compute restaurant bills, salaries, weight loss (or gain), business issues, the fuel efficiency of their cars, who is winning at the Little League game, the cost of each individual item was well as the cart full of food at the grocery store, and thousands of other everyday mundane chores. What does it cost to drive the car four miles to that other grocery store to enjoy their loss leader and save fifty cents on a gallon of milk? Would it make more sense to drive only two miles to my regular grocer and pay the higher price?

Even tasks within tasks require math, such as how many bananas should we buy on a limited budget at the grocery store? We estimate how long they will last relative to the number of people in the household eating them every day.

A miscalculation means that either something is eaten in an overripe condition, thrown out, or must be converted to banana bread to prevent waste. And of course for many families, buying too much of one thing (cigarettes, movie tickets, chocolate candy, beer) may automatically dictate that they buy less of something else (food, rent, electricity, medical or telephone service.)

Likewise, our daily lives are full of mathematical calculations which allow us to make practical decisions. What are my chances of getting into an accident if I'm just driving to the local strip mall? Most accidents happen near home, but do I really need a seat belt if I'm only going a mile away and traveling under thirty-five miles per hour? Do I go through the agonizing effort to reach for the belt, pull it out of its storage place, and fasten it, just to unfasten it in less than five minutes?

And why should I even listen to all the do-gooders who insist I use a seat belt for my own safety? There is a belt law in effect, but what are the chances a cop will see me and want to go to the trouble to stop me and issue a ticket in a residential area?

When I'm on my bicycle or motorcycle, must I follow the law that says I need to wear a helmet? Or if I choose not to, will I be likely to quickly and violently terminate my existence here on Earth, or turn myself into a living vegetable? (If you don't know the correct answer to this, you may not have enough grey matter to spare.)

More complex questions often arise. We are planning a vacation for the kids, or traveling to Grandma's house in another state. Are we safer flying or driving? Recent statistics show that airline travel is far safer that driving or riding in a car, but doesn't that mean the system is overdue for an airline accident? If I fly, which airline is more accident prone? And how long has it been since I was involved in an accident in an automobile? I'm a safe driver, but the other guy may not be. Also, if it is possible, I would rather avoid being on the road on a Friday or Saturday night when all the drunk drivers are out.

There are alternative choices for every situation, and we need to evaluate each to select an acceptable course of action for our circumstances. This is always done using at least a rudimentary form of math. When we think we know instinctively which course has the lowest probability of danger or lowest cost if that is the main issue, then we can make a much more informed decision. That does not preclude us from ultimately choosing a slightly more dangerous course of action for the sake of convenience or lower expense, but at least subconsciously we recognize that there are odds involved. Hopefully, they will always be in our own favor.

Think about your best friend or even a neighbor you dislike. You are not surprised when you see them in the local grocery store. That can easily happen and the odds are very high for this type encounter since you are both in your own neighborhood. It is less likely that you would run into them at a local airport since many people do not regularly frequent that location. But what are the chances of seeing them in the airport of another city, or at a vacation destination, or even among the tens of thousands at Disneyworld?

Clearly, this would be a very unexpected occurrence and you would be quite surprised. The odds of this happening fall even lower the farther away from home you travel.

There are even more esoteric judgments to be made in daily life. Most of us spend a good deal of time outdoors. Do we know what to do when a thunder and lightning storm comes? Do we follow through with the correct action or duck under the nearest tree on the golf course or at the park? You probably don't know the numbers, but every year we hear at least one story about someone who was struck by lightning usually due either to their own carelessness or their lack of knowledge.

What are the odds of us actually dying from a lightning strike? The National Safety Council says that over the course of an entire lifetime for an average person with routine habits, the chances of being killed by a lightning strike are about 1 in 100,000. This is a big number, but not an unmanageable one. Picture a large barrel with 99,999 black plastic marbles in it, and only one white marble. Being blindfolded and reaching into the barrel, you have one chance in 100,000 of picking the white marble. There is not much to gain from such an effort except to understand more clearly the odds of such an unusual event coming to pass. (The odds of dying by a lightning strike in just a single designated year are much longer, at 1 chance in 6,000,000).

Now focus on something more practical concerning the number 100,000. Most homes cost well over $100,000, even after the recent economic turmoil. Many two-income families actually earn more than that in a single year. Also, we are aware of local, state, and national budget issues that involve considerably more than $100,000, and we accept these numbers as representative of something we clearly understand, even if we are unlikely to have an opportunity to put our hands on that kind of money at any time in our lives.

Problems arise in dealing with commas and zeros, however, when we get into even larger numbers. One example is in measuring great distances, such as the distance from the Earth to the sun, the sun being just one of many, many stars in the Milky Way galaxy. Measuring the size of the galaxy itself compounds the issue of keeping track of commas and zeros.

The term "light year" was developed by astronomers to help manage the very numbers associated with measuring distances in space. It refers to the distance light travels in one year, using the standard estimate of the speed of light as 186,000 miles per second.

To put this in perspective, visualize that our Earth revolves around our sun, which is merely a star in the Milky Way that contains around 100 billion stars (and who knows how many planets and moons are there as well). And the Milky Way is about 100,000 light years wide. That number is 100,000 times the distance light travels in one year, at the rate of 186,000 miles per second. That's a pretty big number by any measure. By comparison, the surface of the Earth revolves at about 900 miles an hour, or about 22,000 miles in a full day, or just 10 percent of the distance light travels in a single second.

Over the past two hundred years, science has advanced quite rapidly into areas that generated very large numbers. Besides astronomy, physics, biology, and government spending come to mind quickly. These numbers become so large that they involve a very significant number of commas and zeros. Not surprisingly, the more zeros a number has, the more difficult it is to manipulate. Addition is relatively easy, but other operations such as multiplication get very awkward with so many zeros involved. To compensate for this concern, mathematicians came up with a simple way to handle larger numbers.

This common number, 100,000, can also be written in terms of the power of ten. The power of ten is a technique ordinarily used by scientists and mathematicians to make calculations of very large numbers much easier. The number 100,000 is simply a 1 with five zeros. Mathematicians say this is 1 times 10 to the fifth power, with the five zeros being the fifth power.

It is important to remember for our future discussions that a one with five zeros or 100,000 is the same thing as one times ten to the fifth power. This could also be written as 10^5.

The shorthand for the power of ten came about because mathematicians wanted and needed a simplified way to manipulate the large numbers being generated by modern research. If you wanted to simply multiply 100,000 by 10 you do not need to be a mathematician or a scientist to get 1,000,000, which is the same thing as adding one more zero. That would make 1,000,000 equal to one times ten to the sixth power or 10^6. That was a simple calculation which demonstrates that each additional zero merely adds one more power. When multiplying by ten, the number 10^5 simply becomes 10^6.

Let's examine a more complex but practical case that involves everyday life. Assume the next multi-state lottery drawing for Mega Millions (Powerball is very similar) is a new jackpot because someone won it during the last drawing. It starts again with an initial payout of $10 million. Your odds of winning always remain the same with a single ticket.

Now assume the prize has not been won in some time. There have been a series of drawings with winners identified at all lower levels, but no one has been able to claim the big prize. Each successive jackpot gets larger, even after the government has taken their share. With no big winner the payout has grown, and the next jackpot has increased to the point that it is expected to pay over $100 million or even twice that amount. Jackpots that big would certainly get your attention, but should you buy a ticket? Well, you need to remember that the odds of you winning do not change one iota, just because the pot gets bigger. (The only way to improve your personal odds of winning is to buy more tickets, but each ticket still has the same long individual odds of winning.) Sure, after many many millions of tries, several weeks in a row, someone, somewhere eventually does win the big jackpot, but what are your individual chances if you buy a single ticket?

You instinctively know that they are not very good, regardless of the size of the payout, but just what are the odds?

COL. STEPHEN M. BAUER

Mathematically, the chances of having the winning numbers for the grand prize with a single ticket, as published by both the Mega Millions and the Powerball official websites, are one chance in nearly 200 million or 2×10^8 power. (If you do some research, you will discover that the real odds are slightly lower, so I rounded up to an even number for the sake of simplicity.) Somebody is certainly going to win this jackpot, eventually, but you know it probably isn't going to be you. And remember that the odds of having the winning ticket are exactly the same whether the prize is $10 million for that first drawing after a previous winner, or $100 million or $400 million or more dollars following a long string on drawings with no big winner.

Apply this concept to your own life and the decision making processes you employ every day, usually without even being conscious of it. If I come home late and have to park a car on the crowded street, what are my chances of finding a space near my house? If I call the airline looking for a seat tomorrow morning for a flight, will there be one available in my price range? Have the kids gone next door to play or down the street or several blocks away to a friend's house? If the boss is coming for dinner, should I serve him chicken, beef, pasta, or vegetarian? Does the boss drink white wine, red, nothing strong at all, or possibly even no caffeine? Any decision made or any event that involves making choices includes some level of probability or chance.

Other situations involving chance can be manufactured. What would you think if your grandfather had predicted seventy-five years ago that 1) you would be born, 2) you

would be given the name you have (not even vaguely related to his own name or any known family name), 3) you
would win the Mega Millions or Powerball lottery, and 4)
you would die from a lightning strike? And he said some of
these events would happen in groups like being born and
named, then later winning the lottery and dying at about
the same time?

Does it sound totally and completely preposterous?
Of course it does. Wouldn't most of the family dismiss him
as a crazy lunatic or a liar? Wouldn't he just be judged the
goofy old codger in the corner who must have gotten hold
of some really potent "white lightnin'" brew? Is there any
way remotely possible that he could have made a precisely
correct, wild guess about such things in the future? Or would
everyone assume that his mother dropped him on his head
when he was young? (You may already know a few relatives
or neighbors like that.)

Would it make any difference in terms of such wild
predictions coming to pass if we went farther back in time?
What if your great great great great grandfather had predicted more than one hundred fifty years ago (perhaps from
another country) that you would be born many decades and
generations in the future? And then he said just these two
major events we discussed (being struck by lightning and
winning the big lottery) would happen to you during your
lifetime? That would have been viewed as too crazy to be
given any serious consideration. They would surely have
completely ignored him, or fearing supernatural influences,
locked the old man away, if they let him live at all.

Fortunately for us, calculating the mathematical odds today that both winning the lottery and being hit by lightning would happen to you by pure chance is relatively simple, thanks to modern mathematicians. We only need to multiply the odds of one event happening by the odds of the other event happening. It's that easy. That means we simply multiply one chance in one hundred thousand times one chance in 200 million. This calculation can certainly be done in long hand, but the number of zeros involved gets somewhat unwieldy. This specific circumstance, found often in science, is precisely why mathematicians draw on the power of ten to simplify the exercise.

Using the power of ten, we merely multiply the numbers and add up all the zeros. Calculation of the odds of both events happening is the first event (1×10^5) times the second event (2×10^8). This is done by multiplying the one times the two ($1 \times 2 = 2$), then adding the zeros ($5 + 8 = 13$). It's really that simple.

The probability of your grandfather being right purely by accident is one chance in two times 10^{13} power, or two with thirteen zeros behind it. If you get out a sheet of paper and write this number out in longhand, you will see that it represents one chance in 20 trillion. That is quite a big number, as light only travels about 6 trillion miles in a full year. (Let's not even think about how long it takes government to spend a trillion dollars.)

Assume that grandpa wrote all his predictions down before he passed away, and now we are reading them today. Clearly, lots of folks were thinking back then that this grandpa (or great great great great grandpa) was probably completely off his rocker, but what would these people say if he turned out to be right? And these calculations about the two events, being struck by lightning and winning the lottery, do not even consider the far greater odds that these two events had to happen at the same time, rather than independently at some random point during your lifetime. To pick a specific year for being struck by lightning, we would have to substitute 6 million for the one hundred thousand in our calculations. Furthermore, we have ignored the prediction of when you would be born, and what your name would be. Clearly, that would have upped the odds of one chance in 20 trillion considerably.

History is full of people who have made unusual predictions, sometimes very specific but often rather vague. Most of these are single events, some of which actually happened in some form that can be related to the original prophecy, but many of these events never came to pass. The timing is not always accurate, and the original predictions are often quite fuzzy, but the prognosticators are frequently given credit for having the right idea, while the people who offer this credit usually ignore the missed predictions. Such is the continuing fame attributed to the predictions of Nostradamus, the sixteenth century French apothecary.

Consider the modern-day national forecasts of future hurricanes following the season of Katrina. Predictions of unusually heavy hurricane activity the next year were very far off the mark. And then there is your very enthusiastic local weatherman who has been greatly embarrassed by predicting nine of the last three actual thunderstorms. If one says many times that something is going to happen in the future, and it eventually does, people tend to forget the erroneous predictions, and recall the one that was right. Sure enough, after carrying that umbrella to work for several days, you do eventually need it.

This brings us to the all-important question and the subject of this book: What can modern math teach us about the ancient predictions in the Bible? Is it possible that mathematical calculations might contradict popular scientific judgments about the Bible and the origin of our world? Can we honestly use mathematics to dispute commonly held beliefs so often repeated in the secular media as solid science? More importantly, is Jesus Christ the Messiah spoken of in the Old Testament?

To answer these questions we need to look at a number of statements made in the Bible about future events, examine the evidence showing these events coming to pass, and consider the time frames for the predictions and their fulfillment. Most importantly, what are the odds of each event actually happening purely by accident, and completely independent of each other? And finally, since each event forecasted might be related to the other events forecasted, what is the chance that they could all happen purely by coincidence at about the same time to the same man?

To answer these questions, we need to examine each statement and then assign a probability that it happened purely by accident. To be fair, I will assign what I consider only conservative estimates so as to not artificially increase the overall odds. To determine the possibility that all these events happened to the same person, we will later calculate the odds using the simplified mathematical tool of the power of ten.

Please note that there is no additional calculation made for the possibility that all these events would actually happen at about the same time. That is a major consideration, since any such computation would produce even more astronomical results, and there is virtually no way to even estimate the odds of such a confluence of events. Mentally consider this situation, and adjust your ultimate beliefs accordingly.

40 Prophecies Documented and Fulfilled

THE MESSIAH WOULD BE PRECEDED BY A MESSENGER

PROPHECY by Isaiah about 740 B.C. and Malachi between 450–400 B.C.

> The voice of him that crieth in the wilderness, Prepare ye the way of the LORD, make straight in the desert a highway for our God. . . . And the glory of the LORD shall be revealed, and all flesh shall see it together: for the mouth of the LORD hath spoken it.
>
> —Isaiah 40:3,5

> Behold, I will send my messenger, and he shall prepare the way before me: and the Lord, whom ye seek, shall suddenly come to this temple, even the messenger of the covenant, whom ye delight in: behold, he shall come, saith the LORD of hosts.
>
> —Malachi 3:1

PROPHECY FULFILLED about A.D. 27—These passages foreshadowed the life of a true messenger, John the Baptist, who played an important role in preparing the groundwork for the ministry of Jesus Christ. Jesus was born shortly after John the Baptist about two thousand years ago. Matthew 3:1–2 says:

> In those days came John the Baptist, preaching in the wilderness of Judaea, And saying, Repent ye: for the kingdom of heaven is at hand.

Matthew 11:10–11 confirms the exalted position of John the Baptist here on Earth:

> For this is he, of whom it is written, Behold, I send my messenger before thy face, which shall prepare thy way before thee. Verily I say unto you, Among them that are born of women there hath not risen a greater than John the Baptist: notwithstanding he that is least in the kingdom of heaven is greater than he.

Mark 1:2, Luke 1:76, and Luke 7:27 provide very similar accounts.

Despite the great things John the Baptist did here on Earth, the Bible makes it very clear that he is nevertheless beneath the lowest being in the Kingdom of Heaven.

DISCUSSION OF ODDS: Ordinary people do not have advance messengers go before them. This was a practice employed by high officials to make sure people recognized

COL. STEPHEN M. BAUER

them and were respectful. The chance that there was an advance messenger for the Messiah at first glance seems to be either yes or no, but consider that the messenger not only foretold the coming of the "kingdom of heaven," but he also did it in the wilderness. This suggests that he did not go to the larger villages of the day, which is quite unusual since a large number of people lived in those communities and that would have been the logical place to gather a crowd to listen to him. I say there is 1 chance in 100 this happened by accident.

MATHEMATICAL ODDS—1 in 100 = 1 × 10²

GOD PROMISED ANOTHER PROPHET LIKE MOSES

PROPHECY by Moses about 1450 B.C.

The LORD thy God will raise up unto thee a Prophet from the midst of thee, of thy brethren, like unto me; unto him ye shall hearken; According to all that thou desiredst of the LORD thy God in Horeb in the day of the assembly, saying, Let me not hear again the voice of the LORD my God, neither let me see this great fire any more, that I die not. And the LORD said unto me, They have well spoken that which they have spoken. I will raise them up a Prophet from among their brethren, like unto thee, and will put my words in his mouth; and he shall speak unto them all that I shall command him.

—Deuteronomy 18:15–18

PROPHECY FULFILLED about 5 B.C. to A.D. 30.—Moses told the Jews that God would raise up another prophet like Moses. A succession of prophets followed, including Isaiah, Jeremiah, and Ezekiel, and finally Jesus Christ. Jesus was very much like Moses. Both were delivered from death as infants. Both were prophets. Both performed miracles. Both were leaders. And both were intermediaries between God and man. Of all the prophets, no other prophet is as much like Moses as Jesus. Moses led the Jews out of the bonds of slavery in Egypt into the Promised Land of Israel although Moses died shortly before the Jews actually entered the Promised Land. Jesus leads people—anyone who accepts Him as their Savior—out of the bonds of sin and into the Promised Land of Heaven. Moses offered to die, if God would forgive the sins of the people that Moses was leading (Exodus 32:30–33). Jesus did die for the sins of man, so that people could enter the Kingdom of Heaven.

DISCUSSION OF ODDS—There is little doubt that another prophet "like Moses" would be most extraordinary. Luke quotes the words of the Apostle Peter in Acts 3:20–22 confirmed by his direct witness of Jesus that He was, in fact, the prophet that Moses said was coming.

And he shall send Jesus Christ, which before was preached unto you: Whom the heaven must receive until the times of restitution of all things, which God hath spoken by the mouth of all his holy prophets since the world began. For Moses truly said unto the fathers, A prophet shall the Lord your God raise up unto you of your brethren, like unto me; him shall ye hear in all things whatsoever he shall say unto you.

Jesus Himself went on to claim that He was the one Moses wrote about (John 5:46), and many others affirmed this (John 6:14; 7:40). Moses accomplished so much in his life that another individual would be hard-pressed to match his deeds. But Jesus was in fact like Moses, although He had a much greater impact on mankind and accomplished much more. Of the billions of people who have populated the Earth since the time of Moses, only one has been like him. The odds of this happening are extremely low; I say 1 chance in 1,000,000,000.

MATHEMATICAL ODDS—1 in 1,000,000,000 = 1×10⁹

THE MESSIAH WOULD COME FROM THE TRIBE OF JUDAH

PROPHECY by Moses about 1689 B.C.

> The sceptre shall not depart from Judah, nor a lawgiver from between his feet, until Shiloh come; and unto him shall the gathering of the people be.
> —Genesis 49:10

The scepter is a rod or a staff that is a common accoutrement for any king or ruler. Shiloh is a reference to the Messiah. The authority of the king will be passed down from generation to generation until the Messiah emerges from the tribe of Judah.

PROPHECY FULFILLED about 3 B.C. (or at the birth of Christ)—Abraham was told that the line of promise progressed through his son Isaac and then through Isaac's son, Jacob. Jacob prophesied to his twelve sons that the descendants of Judah will forever be the ones through whom kingship will pass. Therefore, the Messiah must be a descendant of Judah, which He was, as the genealogies in Matthew 1 (for Joseph) and Luke 3 (for Mary) confirm.

There appears to be a conflict here between this prophecy and a curse specified by God in Jeremiah 22:13–30. Both Jehoiakim and his son Coniah (Jeconiah) angered God, who proclaimed that as their punishment absolutely no one from their line of descent would ever rule over the kingdom of Judah ever again. It would appear from the genealogy of Joseph in Matthew 1 that his son, the baby Jesus, would be barred from being the king. It is easy to assume that Satan thought that this would empower him rather than Christ. But we know from other Bible passages that Joseph was not the real father, only the husband of Mary. The real father was God Himself. But somehow the king had to come from the line of Judah. How could that happen? The genealogy in Luke 3 shows clearly that Mary, the mother of Jesus, was in fact a descendent of the line of Judah. God was careful to both fulfill this prophecy of Genesis 49:10 as well as to uphold the curse of Jeconiah (to the great disappointment of Satan).

DISCUSSION OF ODDS—The twelve tribes of Israel were named for the twelve sons of Jacob (Israel), although in some instances the sons of Joseph—Ephraim and Manasseh—were substituted for Joseph, and another tribe was excluded to still total twelve (we will cover this subject in more detail later). That would make the odds one chance in fourteen that the Messiah would come from the tribe of Judah. To simplify the math and make the calculations even more conservative, we'll call it 1 chance in 10.

MATHEMATICAL ODDS—1 in 10 = 1 × 10^1

ISAIAH FORESHADOWED THE VIRGIN BIRTH OF JESUS

PROPHECY by Isaiah about 740 B.C.

> Therefore the Lord himself shall give you a sign; Behold, a virgin shall conceive, and bear a son, and shall call his name Immanuel.
>
> —Isaiah 7:14

It is hard to imagine that someone just dreamed this concept up centuries before Christ was born.

PROPHECY FULFILLED about 3 B.C. (or at the birth of Christ)—Virgin birth (parthenogenesis) is common among plants and lower orders of animals, but not man. Isaiah delivers a unique prophecy that was fulfilled literally with the birth of Jesus about two thousand years ago. Predicting a son rather than a daughter was about a 50/50 guess, but predicting a virgin birth was astonishing. There are several biblical references to Mary being a virgin, and Joseph accepting her status (in an age when premarital sex was quite unusual). Matthew 1:18–24 and Luke 1:27–35 describe the event in considerable detail. Greek mythology also refers often to virgin birth among their gods, but their myths all post-date Isaiah.

DISCUSSION OF ODDS—In the history of the world and the billions of people that have been upon the Earth, no documented proof has ever been offered of any other virgin being pregnant. Since the odds are incalculable, I submit that 1 in 1,000,000,000 is a very conservative estimate of the odds. It is worth noting that Jewish translators use the word "young woman" instead of "virgin," but the authors of the Septuagint, a Greek translation of the Bible written more than two hundred years before Christ, translated this word as "virgin," which was its meaning in biblical Hebrew. At that time, all young women were expected to be virgins, and the moral standards of the day assured everyone that this was in fact the standard conduct for unmarried women. Obviously, exceptions could and undoubtedly were made, and there were some young women who did have premarital sex, but Mary's situation was heavily reported on by people who were in a position to know both her character as well as her activities. No one who offered a written description of both Mary and Joseph even hinted at another alternative other than virgin birth.

MATHEMATICAL ODDS—1 in 1,000,000,000 = 1×10^9

ISAIAH FORESHADOWED THE NAME JESUS WOULD RECEIVE AT HIS BIRTH

PROPHECY by Isaiah about 740 B.C.

> Therefore the Lord himself shall give you a sign; Behold, a virgin shall conceive, and bear a son, and shall call his name Immanuel.
>
> —Isaiah 7:14

> For unto us a child is born, unto us a son is given: and the government shall be upon his shoulder: and his name shall be called Wonderful, Counsellor, The mighty God, The everlasting Father, The Prince of Peace.
>
> —Isaiah 9:6

PROPHECY FULFILLED about 3 B.C. (or at the birth of Christ)—The fact that Mary and Joseph had a son rather than a daughter and named their child "Immanuel," as prophesied makes Isaiah 7:14 two events which are related, but each could have had different circumstances. To maintain a conservative approach, we will treat both as one event. Interestingly, Immanuel which means, "God with us" is quite appropriate because if the Mother is truly a virgin, then He is the Son of God. Because He is the Son of God, Jesus can be accurately referred to as "God with us." Isaiah 9:6 specifically predicts God coming as a man, not a woman.

DISCUSSION OF ODDS—There were hundreds, perhaps

many thousands, of names available to Joseph and Mary, all in common use at the time. Also, it was quite common at the time to name a boy after his father rather than just plucking a completely new and different name out of the air. For example, many have heard the story of Barabbas who was the individual freed by Pilate as the governor of Judea when the crowd selected him rather than Jesus for commutation of his sentence of crucifixion. Jesus was kept in jail and ultimately died on the cross. The name Barabbas in Aramaic literally means the "son of Abba" or the "son of the father." It would not have been at all unusual for Jesus to be named after His father, or for His parents to have selected one of the many thousands of names in common use at the time. The fact that Isaiah identified and predicted that specific name "Immanuel" seven hundred years earlier is extraordinary. Immanuel is not recorded as a common name in history. Conservatively, there is one chance in one thousand that this happened by accident.

MATHEMATICAL ODDS—1 in 1,000 = 1 × 10³

THE MESSIAH WOULD BE BORN IN A VILLAGE CALLED BETHLEHEM

PROPHECY by Micah about 710 B.C.

But thou, Beth-lehem Ephratah, though thou be little among the thousands of Judah, yet out of thee shall he come forth unto me that is to be ruler in Israel; whose goings forth have been from of old, from everlasting.

—Micah 5:2

This prophecy could not be any more straightforward.

PROPHECY FULFILLED about 3 B.C. (or at the birth of Christ)—Approximately seven hundred years earlier, Micah named the tiny village of Bethlehem as the birthplace of Israel's Messiah. The fulfillment of this prophecy in the birth of Christ is one of the most widely known and widely celebrated facts in history. (See Matthew 2:1 and Luke 2:4–7.) What makes the fulfillment of this prophecy even more unusual is the fact that Joseph and Mary were not even living in Bethlehem at the time. Luke 2:1–5 describes how Caesar Augustus ordered everyone to return to their hometown to be taxed. The situation gives every indication that this was a one-time event that was to happen for the first time in this instance. And Joseph and Mary made this seventy mile journey from Nazareth to Bethlehem when she was "great with child." Had this been a routine or repeated requirement, Mary and Joseph would probably have left for Bethlehem at an earlier date when Mary was more comfortable with traveling.

DISCUSSION OF ODDS—Bethlehem is described as a tiny village among the many thousands of villages in Judea. In keeping with the agricultural nature of life during these times, these villages were mostly small, holding at most one hundred fifty to two hundred fifty people, but probably fewer. The world population is estimated to have been from 250 to 300 million souls at that time. They all lived in relatively small farming villages throughout the known world as the concept of cities was foreign to their way of life. There is 1 chance in 1,000,000 that the Messiah would come from this specific small village.

MATHEMATICAL ODDS—1 in 1,000,000 = 1×10^6

Note: When was Christ Jesus born? Read the first few verses of Luke 2 and pay close attention to verses 6–8:

> And so it was, that, while they were there, the days were accomplished that she should be delivered. And she brought forth her firstborn son, and wrapped him in swaddling clothes, and laid him in a manger; because there was no room for them in the inn. And there were in the same country shepherds abiding in the field, keeping watch over their flock by night.

It is worth considering that Caesar Augustus, as thoughtless as he might have been of the welfare of his subjects, probably would not have ordered them to travel in the dead of winter to their own city to be taxed. Citizens that would die while traveling in harsh weather could not pay taxes. It is far more reasonable to believe that everyone was commanded to return to their city to be taxed when the weather was much milder, such as in spring, summer, or fall.

When Joseph took Mary to Bethlehem, she was already "great with child." And at this same time according to verse

8, shepherds were out in their fields watching over their sheep. It was customary that around mid-October, as very cold weather approached, shepherds brought their sheep in from the fields and placed them in some protected area such as a fold. They remained there for the winter, shielded from the harshest elements.

From all of this information, it is reasonable to conclude that Jesus was born at the very least sometime before October, but definitely not during the winter. In fact, there is nothing in the Bible that says when Jesus was born, probably because Christians were not expected to celebrate his birthday.

Jeremiah 10:1–5 speaks to modern Christmas celebrations:

> Hear ye the word which the LORD speaketh unto you, O house of Israel: Thus saith the LORD, Learn not the way of the heathen, and be not dismayed at the signs of heaven; for the heathen are dismayed at them. For the customs of the people are vain: for one cutteth a tree out of the forest, the work of the hands of the workman, with the axe. They deck it with silver and with gold; they fasten it with nails and with hammers, that it move not. They are upright as the palm tree, but speak not: they must needs be borne, because they cannot go. Be not afraid of them; for they cannot do evil, neither also is it in them to do good.

Don't misunderstand my message. I do not see a problem

with celebrating the birth of the Messiah, but we must be careful in how it is done. Many modern Christmas traditions have direct origins in pagan traditions. What is far more important than an estimated date of His birth is recognizing His death, and the great gift that it brought to all of us. We should all celebrate that event, but skip the pagan traditions in the process. My suggestion would be that you wake up every morning and thank God for sending His Son to die for us on the cross. The day Jesus was born cannot be a relevant issue, or the Bible would have told us what day that was.

KINGS WILL BRING HIM GIFTS

PROPHECY by David around 1015 B.C. and by Isaiah about 740 B.C.

> The kings of Tarshish and of the isles shall bring presents: the kings of Sheba and Seba shall offer gifts.
>
> —Psalm 72:10

> The multitude of camels shall cover thee, the dromedaries of Midian and Ephah; all they from Sheba shall come: they shall bring gold and incense; and they shall shew forth the praises of the LORD.
>
> —Isaiah 60:6

PROPHECY FULFILLED about 3 or 4 B.C.
And when they were come into the house, they saw the young child with Mary his mother, and fell down,

and worshipped him: and when they had opened their
treasures, they presented unto him gifts; gold, and frankincense, and myrrh.

—Matthew 2:11

The wise men who followed the star in the east brought
gifts to the baby Jesus, because they perceived Him as a
king. Whether or not the wise men themselves were kings
is debatable, but they were at least representatives of King
Herod. Of course, Herod was jealous of the child that was
to be identified as King of the Jews. He felt that Jesus was
a threat to his own position as king, and he planned to kill
the baby when the wise men reported His location, which
they failed to do after being warned by God.

It is interesting to note that the Bible does not say how
many wise men there were, but it does describe three gifts.
Popular Christian thinking has translated this into there
being three wise men, but it might have easily been two or
four or more travelers looking for the baby who would be
the King of the Jews. Even the prophecy of Psalm 72:10 suggests that there were a minimum of four or more kings who
would recognize the Messiah and offer Him gifts. Nothing
would prevent these kings from bringing more than one gift
made of gold, or frankincense, or myrrh. You may not rely
on a childhood Christmas play to resolve this question. It
is always best to depend on what the Bible says, and in this
case it says nothing about the number of wise men, making
it an irrelevant issue.

DISCUSSION OF ODDS—Gifts in the Bible were generally given to kings or to the temples for the benefit of God. There are examples of gifts being given to sons and daughters or parents, but they are not very common, and that gift-giving is usually within a family. And any example of a gift being given to an infant is rather scarce. For both David and Isaiah who lived more than two centuries apart to have guessed this would happen many centuries in the future, and for it to actually happen entirely by accident, I would say conservatively there is 1 chance in 100.

MATHEMATICAL ODDS 1 in 100 = 1 × 10²

THE SON OF GOD WOULD BE CALLED OUT OF EGYPT IN THE EARLY DAYS OF THE NATION OF ISRAEL

PROPHECY by Hosea between 790–710 B.C.

> When Israel was a child, then I loved him, and called my son out of Egypt.
>
> —Hosea 11:1

PROPHECY FULFILLED about A.D. 1—Before the Son of God could be called out of Egypt, He first had to enter Egypt. And there had to be a reason for Joseph and Mary to travel all the way from Judea to Egypt, more than two hundred miles, with their young son. Matthew 2:13–15 explains:

> And when they were departed, behold, the angel of the Lord appeareth to Joseph in a dream, saying, Arise, and

take the young child and his mother, and flee into Egypt, and be thou there until I bring thee word: for Herod will seek the young child to destroy him. When he arose, he took the young child and his mother by night, and departed into Egypt: And was there until the death of Herod: that it might be fulfilled which was spoken of the Lord by the prophet, saying, Out of Egypt have I called my son.

King Herod had known from his discussions with the wise men that there was a young male child in Israel who was acclaimed as and destined to be the King of the Jews, challenging his throne and the power he held over Israel. He sent the wise men to find Jesus and directed them to report His location. The wise men followed the star to Jesus, but then failed to return to Herod after being warned by God not to return. Herod had intended all along to kill Jesus. Since he could not find Him, the only way he could be sure this was accomplished was to eliminate all boys of that age group. Herod ordered the slaying of all boys two years old and under that lived in Bethlehem and its area. Having been duly warned by God, Joseph and Mary kept Jesus in Egypt until Herod died. It is interesting to note here that some scholars believe it was the young nation of Israel, not Jesus, that was called out of Egypt. Israel was referred to as God's "firstborn" while only Jesus was referred to as the "Son of God," so this prophecy could only relate to the Messiah.

DISCUSSION OF ODDS—Traveling all the way to Egypt (more than two hundred miles) with a small child and staying there until summoned by God is a sequence of events which fulfilled a prophecy made seven centuries earlier. It almost defies human logic that these things happened by accident. I suggest that the odds are at least 1 in 1,000,000 that they happened without the intervention of a supreme being.

MATHEMATICAL ODDS—1 in 1,000,000 = 1 × 10⁶

THE MESSIAH WOULD ANNOUNCE TO ZION IN ADVANCE THAT HE WAS COMING

PROPHECY by Isaiah about 740 B.C.

Behold, the LORD hath proclaimed unto the end of the world, Say ye to the daughter of Zion, Behold, thy salvation cometh; behold, his reward is with him, and his work before him.

—Isaiah 62:11

PROPHECY FULFILLED about A.D. 30—Jesus, knowing that He was the Messiah, commanded two of His disciples to announce to the land of Israel that He was coming.

Tell ye the daughter of Sion, Behold, thy King cometh unto thee, meek, and sitting upon an ass, and a colt the foal of an ass. And the disciples went, and did as Jesus commanded them.

—Matthew 21:5-6

Sion or Zion was the term applied to the Land of Israel and its capital, Jerusalem. Zion is also the name of a mountain where King David conquered a Jebusite fortress, resulting in the place being renamed the City of David. At the time, the City of David was Bethlehem. The term also refers to what is known today as Old Jerusalem. This was the center of the Jewish population and the focus of religious activity during that day. As a practical matter, it is somewhat surprising that Jerusalem in both the past and the present commands so much attention. It is not a seaport. It is not located on any major waterway, does not sit astride any major historic trade route, and has no appreciable mineral wealth to demand attention. Yet, it is the focus of world attention today, and is also the focus of world events to come as described in the book of Revelation. It is because God said it would be, and He knew because He is not constrained by our time dimension. More on this issue later.

DISCUSSION OF ODDS—Jesus knew that He must fulfill this prophecy if He was the Messiah, so I would assign a high probability that this would happen by design rather than pure chance. I say there is 1 chance in 10 this happened by accident.

MATHEMATICAL ODDS—1 in 10 = 1 x 10^1

THE MESSIAH WOULD BE PRESENTED TO THE WORLD IN 483 YEARS

PROPHECY by Daniel about 538 B.C.

Know therefore and understand, that from the going
forth of the commandment to restore and to build Jerusalem unto the Messiah the Prince shall be seven weeks,
and threescore and two weeks: the street shall be built
again, and the wall, even in troublous times.

—Daniel 9:25

PROPHECY FULFILLED about A.D. 30—Daniel foretold
the day that Christ would enter Jerusalem as the Messiah.
The prophecy refers to sixty-nine weeks of years (69 × 7 =
483 years) after the decree to rebuild Jerusalem, until His
coming. This is calculated using the Babylonian 360-day
calendar, since Daniel was written in Babylon during the
Jewish captivity after the fall of Jerusalem. To make this
calculation, we need to use the Jewish calendar which
has 360 days, not the 365 days in the Gregorian calendar.
Therefore, 483 years × 360 days = 173,880 days. Records
found by Sir Henry Creswicke Rawlinson in the Shushan
(Susa) Palace, and confirmed in Nehemiah 2:1, show this
decree was apparently offered on March 14, 445 B.C., by
Artaxerxes Longimanus to the Hebrew priest Ezra. Exactly
173,880 days later, on April 6, 30 A.D., Jesus Christ entered
Jerusalem riding a donkey. This day is now celebrated as
Palm Sunday. The following week, Christ was crucified.

DISCUSSION OF ODDS—Clearly, this is an elaborate calculation, and other versions of this prophecy offer different
dates using 365 day years, even correcting for leap years. It
is important to note that Daniel made his prophecy more
than five hundred years earlier and it contained a critical

milestone. The appearance of the Messiah had to occur 483 years after a specific event which itself was to happen in the future. He could have been wrong, but since Daniel made his prophecy nearly one million days ago, the only person with a credible claim to being the Messiah was Jesus Christ. Daniel's selection of that specific time frame, even if the various versions offer calculations that are off by a few days, is therefore 1 chance in 1,000,000. The more time that passes without having any other man make a credible claim to being the Messiah makes the odds even longer.

MATHEMATICAL ODDS—1 in 1,000,000 = 1 × 10^6

GOD WILL OFFER A SERVANT WHO WILL BE A SALVATION TO ALL, BUT WILL AVOID ATTENTION.

PROPHECY by Isaiah about 712 B.C.

> Behold my servant, whom I uphold; mine elect, in whom my soul delighteth; I have put my spirit upon him: he shall bring forth judgment to the Gentiles. He shall not cry, nor lift up, nor cause his voice to be heard in the street.
> —Isaiah 42:1–2

PROPHECY FULFILLED about A.D. 30—Isaiah was quite accurate in foretelling how Jesus, as the servant of God and the salvation for all men, would try not to draw attention to Himself.

Then the Pharisees went out, and held a council against him, how they might destroy him. But when Jesus knew it, he withdrew himself from thence: and great multitudes followed him, and he healed them all; And charged them that they should not make him known.

—Matthew 12:14–16

Clearly, Jesus did not want to advertise Himself as the Messiah. He gave specific instructions to the people who had already seen Him perform miracles of healing. He probably knew they could not contain their excitement and joy at having seen such awesome deeds done, but He nevertheless gave them every indication that He wished to remain anonymous.

DISCUSSION OF ODDS—Could Isaiah have known seven hundred years earlier that the Messiah would have occasion to want to escape attention and not draw notice to Himself? Ordinarily, anyone with a message to proclaim to the masses would work very hard to draw attention to themselves and their message. And they at least hope (if they don't directly ask) that every one who hears them pass the message of salvation on to others who were not there. Word of mouth helps carry the point farther, but Jesus went out of His way to avoid this kind of publicity. This is contradictory to the basic effort to educate the public, and it is doubtful that this happened by accident, although everyone might do it at one time or another. I submit there is one chance in 100 that this happened by accident and Isaiah just guessed that it would.

MATHEMATICAL ODDS—1 in 10 = 1 × 10²

THE MESSIAH WILL SPEAK IN PARABLES REVEALING FUNDAMENTAL TRUTHS

PROPHECY by Asaph about 1,000 B.C.

> Give ear, O my people, to my law: incline your ears to the words of my mouth. I will open my mouth in a parable: I will utter dark sayings of old.
>
> —Psalm 78:1–2

PROPHECY FULFILLED about A.D. 30—The books of Matthew, Mark, Luke, and John describe various parables in considerable detail.

> All these things spake Jesus unto the multitude in parables; and without a parable spake he not unto them.
>
> —Matthew 13:34

> And with many such parables spake he the word unto them, as they were able to hear it. But without a parable spake he not unto them: and when they were alone, he expounded all things to his disciples.
>
> —Mark 4:33–34

DISCUSSION OF ODDS—The Bible tells a great number of stories which describe historical events, and of course it also offers prophecies of future events to come. Parables are different in that they are meant to be teaching points describing imaginary situations which result in a moral or philosophical point of view on life and how it should be lived. The difference between real historical events and parables is that real names are used for things that actually happened, and parables refer to "a man" or "a woman" without using a name. The reader is left with an understanding of what is right and what is wrong in particular situations but we cannot document the facts since names are excluded. The concept of parables is a little unusual but not out of the question since anecdotes have always been around. Even today, great pronouncements are made by political leaders that cite anecdotal evidence of some lesson to be learned. I would assign odds of one chance in 10 that Asaph, an obscure music leader and teacher in the court of King David, would just guess this would happen.

MATHEMATICAL ODDS—1 in 10 = 1 × 10¹

THE MESSIAH WOULD PERFORM HEALING MIRACLES

PROPHECY by Isaiah about 713 B.C.

Then the eyes of the blind shall be opened, and the ears of the deaf shall be unstopped. Then shall the lame man leap as an hart, and the tongue of the dumb sing: for in the wilderness shall waters break out, and streams in the desert.

—Isaiah 35:5-6

PROPHECY FULFILLED about A.D. 29

And Jesus departed from thence, and came nigh unto the sea of Galilee; and went up into a mountain, and sat down there. And great multitudes came unto him, having with them those that were lame, blind, dumb, maimed, and many others, and cast them down at Jesus' feet; and he healed them: Insomuch that the multitude wondered, when they saw the dumb to speak, the maimed to be whole, the lame to walk, and the blind to see: and they glorified the God of Israel.

—Matthew 15:29-31

Mark 7:31-37 and Luke 7:20-22 are just two more examples which document the numerous times that Jesus healed various infirmities for a large number of people. Healing such as this had never been seen before or since, except possibly for the intervention of modern medicine. These are the type of events that would be screaming headlines if they were to happen today.

DISCUSSION OF ODDS—This prophecy really has two parts. Could Isaiah have known centuries earlier that the Messiah would be a healer? And could anyone really heal people of these type infirmities? The simple answer is that no man could know this in advance, and no man could perform these acts of healing without the intervention of a divine God. The eyewitness accounts of His healing ability also record a substantial number of witnesses. I would estimate that the odds of both these events happening by accident are 1 in 1,000,000.

MATHEMATICAL ODDS—1 in 1,000,000 = 1 × 10⁶

THE MESSIAH WOULD ENTER JERUSALEM WHILE RIDING ON A DONKEY

PROPHECY by Zechariah between 520–518 B.C.

> Rejoice greatly, O daughter of Zion; shout, O daughter of Jerusalem: behold, thy King cometh unto thee: he is just, and having salvation; lowly, and riding upon an ass, and upon a colt the foal of an ass.
>
> —Zechariah 9:9

PROPHECY FULFILLED about A.D. 30—More than five hundred years before Christ entered Jerusalem, Zechariah spoke of a future king presenting himself to the city while riding on a humble donkey. As explained in Matthew 21:2–11, Mark 11:2–11, Luke 19:35–37, and John 12:14–15, Jesus both rode into Jerusalem on a donkey and then presented Himself to all the people as the Messiah, the King.

DISCUSSION OF ODDS—Although it was not unusual

for someone to ride a donkey, or even a camel or horse, the most popular form of transportation at that time was to walk. And up to this point in His life and ministry, Jesus had gone just about everywhere on foot, not riding on an animal. Most movements in the Bible refer to individuals walking rather than riding, but a conservative estimate is that there was one chance in ten that He would enter Jerusalem riding on a donkey.

MATHEMATICAL ODDS—1 in 10 = 1 × 10^1

MEN WOULD HEAP SCORN ON THE MESSIAH

PROPHECY by David around 1000 B.C.

> All they that see me laugh me to scorn: they shoot out the lip, they shake the head saying, He trusted on the LORD that he would deliver him: let him deliver him, seeing he delighted in him.
>
> —Psalm 22:7–8

PROPHECY FULFILLED about A.D. 30

> And they that passed by reviled him, wagging their heads, And saying, Thou that destroyest the temple, and buildest it in three days, save thyself. If thou be the Son of God, come down from the cross. Likewise also the chief

priests mocking him, with the scribes and elders, said, He saved others; himself he cannot save. If he be the King of Israel, let him now come down from the cross, and we will believe him. He trusted in God; let him deliver him now, if he will have him: for he said, I am the Son of God. The thieves also, which were crucified with him, cast the same in his teeth.

—Matthew 27:39–44

Many people who did not see Jesus perform miracles did disparage and ridicule Him. The chief priests were probably the most vocal of the bunch in that they had the most to lose from any public recognition of His deity. Some went so far as to challenge Him when He was hanging on the cross to come down on His own, if He were truly the chosen one.

DISCUSSION OF ODDS—It is probably not so extraordinary for men in general to be scornful toward someone who is accused of a crime. It is basic human nature, and men have done this throughout history. The legal system in America recognized this tendency, making the modern point that any accused person should be considered innocent until proven guilty. Despite this admonishment, even today many people assume that someone charged with a crime is guilty, or they would not have been charged. Of course, proving their guilt is something else altogether, and even jury trials pronounce the accused either guilty or not guilty, but juries do not say someone is innocent. In this case, the local government officials participated in this scorn of Jesus which is a little more unusual in that they were the ones who were responsible for being objective, or so it would appear. I say the odds are one in ten this happened by accident.

MATHEMATICAL ODDS—1 in 10 = 1 × 10¹

THE ESTABLISHMENT LEADERS WOULD CONSPIRE TO KILL THE MESSIAH

PROPHECY by David around 1000 B.C.

> Why do the heathen rage, and the people imagine a vain thing? The kings of the earth set themselves, and the rulers take counsel together, against the LORD, and against his anointed, saying, Let us break their bands asunder, and cast away their cords from us.
>
> —Psalm 2:1–3

PROPHECY FULFILLED about A.D. 30—Both Matthew and Luke describe this event in precise detail.

> Ye know that after two days is the feast of the passover, and the Son of man is betrayed to be crucified. Then assembled together the chief priests, and the scribes, and the elders of the people, unto the palace of the high priest, who was called Caiaphas, And consulted that they might take Jesus by subtilty, and kill him.
>
> —Matthew 26:2–4

Now the feast of unleavened bread drew nigh, which is called the Passover. And the chief priests and scribes sought how they might kill him; for they feared the people.

—Luke 22:1–2

DISCUSSION OF ODDS—It is almost inconceivable that God would send a man to Earth who could demonstrate such supernatural powers as to perform all the miracles that He did, and then men would not fear Him. Even more important, they apparently did not fear the one who sent Him. But these religious leaders were quite afraid that they were about to lose control of the masses and they would cede power over the people to someone new. This was as unacceptable to them then, as the notion would be to most politicians today. I would say that there is one chance in 100 that they would take such a drastic course of action as a routine response to such an incredible display of power and majesty.

MATHEMATICAL ODDS—1 in 100 = 1 × 10²

FALSE WITNESSES WILL RISE AGAINST THE MESSIAH

PROPHECY by David around 1000 B.C.

Deliver me not over unto the will of mine enemies: for

false witnesses are risen up against me, and such as breathe out cruelty.

—Psalm 27:12

PROPHECY FULFILLED about A.D. 30

Now the chief priests, and elders, and all the council, sought false witness against Jesus, to put him to death; But found none: yea, though many false witnesses came, yet found they none. At the last came two false witnesses, And said, This fellow said, I am able to destroy the temple of God, and to build it in three days.

—Matthew 26:59–61

And the chief priests and all the council sought for witness against Jesus to put him to death; and found none. For many bare false witness against him, but their witness agreed not together. And there arose certain, and bare false witness against him. . . .

—Mark 14:55–57

David foresaw a thousand years before Christ that it would be necessary to bring false witnesses against the Savior. They did not all share the same story, but their accounts condemned Jesus, and were just what the chief priests were looking for.

DISCUSSION OF ODDS—False witnesses are not uncommon, even today. People who are charged with a crime that they are guilty of, often enlist the support of others to divert attention or create an alibi. However, it is much rarer that government officials will go out of their way to create false witnesses and convict someone of a crime, although that too happens occasionally. I give it one chance in 10 that this happened by accident to Christ.

MATHEMATICAL ODDS—1 in 10 = 1 × 10¹

JESUS WOULD KNOW IN ADVANCE THAT A TRUSTED FRIEND WOULD BETRAY HIM

PROPHECY by David around 1000 B.C.

> Yea, mine own familiar friend, in whom I trusted, which did eat of my bread, hath lifted up his heel against me.
> —Psalm 41:9

PROPHECY FULFILLED about A.D. 30—Psalm 41 begins by talking about the one who helps the poor, and how the Lord will eventually deliver him in time of trouble. Jesus, during His time on Earth, and even more so following His crucifixion has arguably done more to help the poor than any man in history. Both Matthew and John describe how Jesus was aware that one of His friends would betray Him, but David told of it a thousand years earlier.

And as they did eat, he said, Verily I say unto you, that

one of you shall betray me. And they were exceeding sorrowful, and began every one of them to say unto him, Lord, is it I? And he answered and said, He that dippeth his hand with me in the dish, the same shall betray me.

—Matthew 26:21–23

I speak not of you all: I know whom I have chosen: but that the scripture may be fulfilled, He that eateth bread with me hath lifted up his heel against me. Now I tell you before it come, that, when it is come to pass, ye may believe that I am he.

—John 13:18–19

DISCUSSION OF ODDS—It is quite interesting that not only did David foresee that Jesus would know in advance that He would be betrayed by a friend, but He anticipated that the friend would also eat dinner with Him before he betrayed Him. (That is really two prophecies we are treating as one.) It is also quite interesting that Jesus was aware of what would happen and offered the prophecy to His disciples as a way of further convincing them that He was the Messiah. By telling them in advance, He was demonstrating that He knew the future, and even though He revealed it directly to someone who would fulfill the prophecy, they were unable to restrain themselves and avoid betraying Him. I suggest that the odds of these events happening by chance are one in 100.

MATHEMATICAL ODDS—1 in 100 = 1×10^2

THE MESSIAH WOULD BE BETRAYED BY A FRIEND

PROPHECY by David 1000 B.C.

> Yea, mine own familiar friend, in whom I trusted, which did eat of my bread, hath lifted up his heel against me.
>
> —Psalm 41:9

PROPHECY FULFILLED about A.D. 30

> And while he yet spake, lo, Judas, one of the twelve, came, and with him a great multitude with swords and staves, from the chief priests and elders of the people. Now he that betrayed him gave them a sign, saying, Whomsoever I shall kiss, that same is he: hold him fast. And forthwith he came to Jesus, and said, Hail, master; and kissed him. And Jesus said unto him, Friend, wherefore art thou come? Then came they, and laid hands on Jesus, and took him.
>
> —Matthew 26:47–50

Other accounts of the betrayal of Jesus by His friend are recorded in Mark 14:43–46, Luke 22:47–48, and John 18:2–5.

DISCUSSION OF ODDS—Jesus had performed many miracles in the presence of His disciples and they had gone to great lengths to stop what they were doing and follow Him. Their devotion to Him was exceptionally strong by the time they had partaken of the last supper, so it seems very unusual that one of them would betray Him. He did not speak of betrayal in a general sense from someone He knew, but specifically identified the betrayer. Still, He was betrayed. Although they were essentially quite poor, the money involved was somewhat of an attraction, so I'd suggest there was one chance in 10 that one of His own would betray Him.

MATHEMATICAL ODDS—1 in 10 = 1 × 10¹

THE MESSIAH WOULD BE DESPISED AND BE REJECTED

PROPHECY by Isaiah about 712 B.C.

> He is despised and rejected of men; a man of sorrows, and acquainted with grief: and we hid as it were our faces from him; he was despised, and we esteemed him not.
> —Isaiah 53:3

PROPHECY FULFILLED about A.D. 30—The gospels of Matthew, Mark, Luke, and John describe in great detail how the Messiah suffered and was despised and rejected, not only by the Jews, but by the Romans, the gentiles, and even His own disciples for a short time. Numerous stories tell of the continuous persecution of Christ by the high priests, government officials, the general public, and even His close friends and disciples. This type of treatment is usually reserved for the vilest members of a community. Even when one faction decides they reject an individual, it is not at all uncommon for another faction to disagree with them. To have all of these parties acting against Christ is quite unusual given that all He had done was perform numerous miracles and preach salvation for all mankind.

DISCUSSION OF ODDS—It's easy to understand how the Romans rejected Jesus. They did not want any competition to their authority over the populace from a strong leader for the Jews. The chief priests fall into the same category. The gentiles were largely tuned out from the prophecies of the Jewish holy books, so they might easily have found fault with Jesus. It is a little harder to understand how the Jews could reject Christ as the Messiah, after considering all the evidence of early prophecy in the Jewish holy books and ultimately in the Bible—prophecies which He fulfilled in great detail. And it is very hard to understand how some of the disciples could reject Christ after all the miracles they had witnessed, even if their rejection was very temporary. I say the odds are one in 1,000.

MATHEMATICAL ODDS—1 in 1,000 = 1 × 10³

THE MESSIAH WILL BEAR ALL OUR BURDENS AND TRANSGRESSIONS, AND WHEN HE IS WHIPPED WE WILL BE HEALED

PROPHECY by Isaiah about 712 B.C.

Surely he hath borne our griefs, and carried our sorrows: yet we did esteem him stricken, smitten of God, and afflicted. But he was wounded for our transgressions, he was bruised for our iniquities: the chastisement of our peace was upon him; and with his stripes we are healed. All we like sheep have gone astray; we have turned every one to his own way; and the LORD hath laid on him the iniquity of us all.

—Isaiah 53: 4–6

PROPHECY FULFILLED about A.D. 30—The crucifixion of Christ illustrated in Matthew, Mark, Luke, and John amply describes how He accepted the punishing torture of the cross to atone for all the sins of mankind. This included all the sins of man committed before His death, and also for all the sins of man that would be committed on Earth in the future. The reference to the stripes is a direct reference to Christ being beaten with a leather whip tipped with iron barbs. This is an integral part of the entire process the Messiah had to go through before we could have salvation offered to us.

DISCUSSION OF ODDS—Non-believers will question whether or not Christ died for our sins, but it is clear from several accounts that Christ was tortured and whipped with leather straps that had iron barbs attached to the tips of the leather straps. This caused unbelievable trauma, inflicting deep cuts in the skin and muscles, and resulting in enormous pain and suffering. Isaiah might have guessed (seven hundred years earlier) this would happen, but I'd say there was one chance in a million that it was a random event.

MATHEMATICAL ODDS—1 in 1,000,000 = 1 × 10⁶

MEN WILL SPEAK WELL OF THE MESSIAH AND WANT TO BE WITH HIM, BUT THEIR HEARTS WILL NOT BE WITH HIM

PROPHECY by Isaiah and Ezekiel 712–587 B.C.

Wherefore the Lord said, Forasmuch as this people draw near me with their mouth, and with their lips do honour me, but have removed their heart far from me, and their fear toward me is taught by the precept of men.

—Isaiah 29:13

And they come unto thee as the people cometh, and they sit before thee as my people, and they hear thy words, but they will not do them: for with their mouth they shew much love, but their heart goeth after their covetousness.

—Ezekiel 33:31

PROPHECY FULFILLED about A.D. 30—Jesus Himself told of the hypocrisy of many of the people who went to Him, followed Him, and complimented Him with kind remarks, but secretly followed another moral code.

Ye hypocrites, well did Esaias prophesy of you, saying, This people draweth nigh unto me with their mouth, and honoureth me with their lips; but their heart is far from me. But in vain they do worship me, teaching for doctrines the commandments of men.

—Matthew 15:7–9

Mark 7:6–7 recounts the same events.

Interestingly enough, in documenting the fulfillment of this prophecy, Jesus takes the opportunity to condemn those who create their own form of religious doctrine to follow. Everyone should be careful to insure that their religious compass points to the teachings of the Son of God, and not some modern interpretation made by man. This issue is the root cause of many of the modern versions of the Bible and sidetracks in doctrinal interpretation. People with an agenda reinterpret the words of God to satisfy their own desires. Just one example is Dr. Virginia Mollenkott, an acknowledged lesbian, who assisted in the translation of the New International Version of the Bible. Comparing passages from the historically accepted King James Version to the NIV will show clearly that Dr. Mollenkott, along with other members of the translation committee, watered down the condemnation of this sexual practice. Clearly, their intention was to convince modern man that their own lifestyle was not condemned by God.

DISCUSSION OF ODDS—Throughout history people have been drawn to power. They want to know political leaders and be known by them. They want to be seen with movie and music stars, and some people will do anything to be photographed with them. They want to be around the rich and the famous as though some of their advantages might rub off on the more unfortunate. Or at the least they can impress their friends. Certainly, many of these followers are in perfect sync with the objects of their adulation. Fawning over politicians and celebrities does not always mean that the people endorse them or their publicly stated positions. I would assign odds of one chance in 10 that this happened by accident.

MATHEMATICAL ODDS—1 in 10 = 1×10^1

ZECHARIAH SPOKE OF THE BETRAYAL OF JESUS FOR THIRTY PIECES OF SILVER

PROPHECY by Zechariah between 520–518 B.C.

> And I said unto them, If ye think good, give me my price; and if not, forbear. So they weighed for my price thirty pieces of silver.
>
> —Zechariah 11:12

PROPHECY FULFILLED about A.D. 30

> Then one of the twelve, called Judas Iscariot, went unto the chief priests, And said unto them, What will ye give me, and I will deliver him unto you? And they covenanted with him for thirty pieces of silver.
>
> —Matthew 26:14–15

These verses explain that Judas was paid specifically thirty silver coins for his betrayal of Jesus. Judas told the Romans where they could arrest Jesus without having to deal with a crowd of Jesus' followers, making it much easier for them to take Him captive without arousing the public. What makes this prophecy particularly unique is the very precise number of pieces of silver.

DISCUSSION OF ODDS—To be betrayed by a friend is not so unusual, because by definition betrayal comes from a friend, not a stranger. But to be betrayed for a very specific amount of money is quite unique. The betrayal could have been for a favor, or forbearance of an act, for food, lodging, some appointment to power, or anything of value. But to be betrayed specifically for thirty pieces of silver, as opposed to any other quantity of silver or for some amount of gold or something else of value is rather unusual. I suggest that conservatively there is less than one chance in 100,000 that more than five hundred years before, Zechariah got the fact of the betrayal, the exact number of coins paid, and the type of metal (gold or silver) correct.

MATHEMATICAL ODDS—1 in 100,000 = 1×10^5

ZECHARIAH SPOKE OF THE THIRTY PIECES OF SILVER BEING CAST TO A POTTER

PROPHECY by Zechariah between 520–518 B.C.

And the LORD said unto me, Cast it unto the potter: a goodly price that I was prised at [valued by] of them. And I took the thirty pieces of silver, and cast them to the potter in the house of the LORD.

—Zechariah 11:13

PROPHECY FULFILLED about A.D. 30—Matthew 27:3–7 explains that after Judas received thirty pieces of silver to betray Jesus, he felt exceedingly guilty for his betrayal, so he tossed the money into the temple (the house of the Lord) and then hung himself. Not wanting to keep this "dirty" money in the temple treasury, the chief priests used it to buy a potter's field as a burial place for the poor.

Then Judas, which had betrayed him, when he saw that he was condemned, repented himself, and brought again the thirty pieces of silver to the chief priests and elders, Saying, I have sinned in that I have betrayed the innocent blood. And they said, What is that to us? see thou to that. And he cast down the pieces of silver in the temple, and departed, and went and hanged himself. And the chief priests took the silver pieces, and said, It is not lawful for to put them into the treasury, because it is the price of blood. And they took counsel, and bought with them the potter's field, to bury strangers in.

DISCUSSION OF ODDS—The fact that Judas ultimately became overwrought with guilt over the money he took to betray Jesus is unusual, but he had many options to rid himself of the evidence. He might have given the money to a poor family member. He might have given it to a poor stranger or some beggar along the road. He might have just thrown it away in the bushes, or even given it to Jesus to make some amends for his duplicity. But he elected to give it back to the chief priests who gave it to him. In the process, he was so overcome with remorse that he did not even take the time to actually hand the thirty pieces of silver to them. It is most unusual for a contribution to a temple to be thrown in, rather than being handed in or sent by a messenger. Even today, many people are quite demonstrative about their giving, wanting everyone within sight or hearing to know how much they have done for the church. Also, there are so many options the priests could have exercised to put the thirty pieces of silver to use, it almost defies logic to think that they would select the option predicted by Zechariah more than five hundred years earlier. I estimate there is much less than one chance in 1,000,000 that they would buy a potter's field.

MATHEMATICAL ODDS—1 in 1,000,000 = 1 × 10⁶

THE MESSIAH WOULD BE SILENT BEFORE HIS ACCUSERS

PROPHECY by Isaiah about 712 B.C.

He was oppressed, and he was afflicted, yet he opened not

his mouth: he is brought as a lamb to the slaughter, and as a sheep before her shearers is dumb, so he openeth not his mouth.

—Isaiah 53:7

PROPHECY FULFILLED about A.D. 30—Matthew 27:12–14 explains that when Jesus was accused by the chief priests and the elders, and they invited Him to tell His side of the story, He gave no answer. The governor Pilate then asked Jesus, "Don't you hear the testimony they are bringing against you?" Jesus made no reply whatsoever, to the great amazement of the governor. John 19:9–10 says:

And went again into the judgment hall, and saith unto Jesus, Whence art thou? But Jesus gave him no answer. Then saith Pilate unto him, Speakest thou not unto me? knowest thou not that I have power to crucify thee, and have power to release thee?

DISCUSSION OF ODDS—Throughout history, there have been many millions of people accused of capital crimes. It is very difficult to imagine that someone so charged, knowing full well that the ultimate punishment was at stake, would not offer at least a few words of defense. Even a guilty person will offer some story (no matter how outrageous their tale) of how they are innocent. But the innocent always offer a defense, having nothing to lose by being honest. I suggest the odds of an innocent man (especially the most innocent man who ever walked the Earth) accused of a capital crime offering not a single word in self defense is non-existent, but at the very least, one chance in 100,000,000.

MATHEMATICAL ODDS—1 in 100,000,000 = 1 × 10⁸

THE MESSIAH WOULD BE SPIT UPON AND BEATEN

PROPHECY by Isaiah about 712 B.C.

> I gave my back to the smiters, and my cheeks to them that plucked off the hair: I hid not my face from shame and spitting.
>
> —Isaiah 50:6

The book of Isaiah is named for the prophet who first addresses God's judgment for those who refuse to repent and turn to Him. The first thirty-nine chapters are primarily focused on Israel and the judgment it will receive. From chapter forty on, Isaiah addresses the issue of salvation through the Messiah.

PROPHECY FULFILLED about A.D. 30—Matthew 26:67–68 describes how the scribes and the elders who comprised the council of Caiaphas spit in Jesus' face and struck Him with their fists after the high priest declared that He had spoken blasphemy. Others slapped Him and said, "Prophesy unto us, thou Christ, Who is he that smote thee?" Note that the prophecy was for the hair to be plucked from

His cheeks, meaning they tore off His beard, undoubtedly disfiguring Him. We will see later how His own disciple did not recognize Him after His resurrection, apparently from the severe damage that had been done to His face. Jesus was beaten, mocked, and taunted before His crucifixion by the Romans. Mark 14:65, Luke 22:62–63, and John 19:3 also describe this event.

DISCUSSION OF ODDS—Transgressors were routinely punished by the priests, and certainly many were put to death. However, it was very unusual to have an accused suffer all the pain, torture, and public humiliation that Jesus endured prior to His crucifixion. Torture itself can take a very wide variety of forms. History is full of gruesome acts employed in the process of inflicting pain on others. Having the beard pulled off one's face has to rank fairly high on any list of the most unusual methods employed. I suggest the odds are one in 100,000 that this would have happened by chance.

MATHEMATICAL ODDS—1 in 100,000 = 1 × 10^5

HE WOULD HAVE HIS HANDS AND FEET PIERCED

PROPHECY by David 1000 B.C.

For dogs have compassed me: the assembly of the wicked have inclosed me: they pierced my hands and my feet.
—Psalm 22:16

David offers a very descriptive prayer of despair.

PROPHECY FULFILLED about A.D. 30—Accounts in Matthew 27:38, Mark 15:27, Luke 23:32, and John 19:18 describe various aspects of the crucifixion of Christ. This of course included the piercing of His hands and His feet with nails, as was customary in Roman executions, fulfilling a prophecy made a thousand years earlier.

DISCUSSION OF ODDS—Crucifixion was commonly practiced from the sixth century B.C. until the fourth century A.D., when it was finally abolished in A.D. 337 by Constantine I. It was intended to serve as both a severe punishment for the convicted individual and a frightful deterrent to others, as these were always carried out in public venues. At the time, crucifixion was unanimously considered the most horrible form of death known to man. David foretold of the crucifixion of the Messiah at a time in history when it was virtually unheard of. I suggest the odds are one in 10,000 that he could have accidentally anticipated such a cruel death.

MATHEMATICAL ODDS—1 in 10,000 = 1 × 10^4

ZECHARIAH FORETOLD OF THE WOUNDS IN THE MESSIAH'S HANDS, CAUSED BY HIS FRIENDS

PROPHECY by Zechariah between 520–518 B.C.

And one shall say unto him, What are these wounds in

thine hands? Then he shall answer, Those with which I was wounded in the house of my friends.

—Zechariah 13:6

Zechariah opens chapter thirteen by prophesying that there will be "a fountain opened to the house of David and to inhabitants of Jerusalem for sin and for uncleanness." This might be considered a separate prophecy, but the fountain would obviously be the Messiah.

PROPHECY FULFILLED about A.D. 30—The accounts in Matthew 27:38, Mark 15:27, Luke 23:32, and John 19:18 describe how Christ was nailed to the cross (by His hands and His feet). Related verses explain how He was with friends, and what they did to insure that He would be killed in such an unusual manner. Later, He revealed His wounds to the disciples, but Thomas was skeptical and asked about the wounds to be sure of the claims made by Jesus. This uncertainty gave rise to the notion of a "doubting Thomas."

DISCUSSION OF ODDS—Once again, because crucifixion was unknown five centuries before Christ was nailed to the cross, there is simply no way that Zechariah could have known five hundred years in advance that Jesus would be wounded in such a way, at the hands of friends, and that He would be asked to explain them. This is another case of multiple prophecies that we will treat as one, knowing that the odds of several things happening simultaneously are actually much higher. I say conservatively there is one chance in 1,000 that he could have guessed this, and it would come to pass accidentally.

GOD'S SERVANT WOULD BE CRUCIFIED WITH CRIMINALS

PROPHECY by Isaiah about 712 B.C.

> Therefore will I divide him a portion with the great, and he shall divide the spoil with the strong; because he hath poured out his soul unto death: and he was numbered with the transgressors; and he bare the sin of many. . . .
> —Isaiah 53:12

PROPHECY FULFILLED about A.D. 30—Mark.15:27 describes this perfectly:

> And with him they crucify two thieves; the one on his right hand, and the other on his left.

Matthew 27:38 offers almost exactly the same narrative, confirming that Christ was punished among the other common transgressors of the day.

DISCUSSION OF ODDS—Jesus was certainly numbered with the transgressors. He could have been executed alone, or with only one other, but His death fulfilled a prophecy made seven hundred years earlier. There is one chance in 10 that this situation happened by accident.

MATHEMATICAL ODDS—1 in 10 = 1 × 10¹

GOD'S SERVANT WOULD PRAY FOR HIS TORMENTORS

PROPHECY by Isaiah about 712 B.C.

. . . he bare the sin of many, and made intercession for the transgressors.

—Isaiah 53:12

PROPHECY FULFILLED about A.D. 30

Then said Jesus, Father, forgive them; for they know not what they do. . . .

—Luke 23:34

Jesus offered a very specific prayer to God for His executioners, begging the Father to forgive those who tortured and killed Him.

DISCUSSION OF ODDS—The Christian religion has produced a significant number of individuals who have prayed for their executioners. These people were inspired by Christ Himself, but before Christ's time and before the great example He set, very few if any people dying by torture would ask God to forgive the ones responsible for their own deaths. In fact, there are no records of anyone acting in such a manner before Christ set the example. It would be much more likely that anyone about to die would either silently or publicly curse those responsible, if they were not actively begging for a reprieve. I suggest there is only one chance in 100,000 that this would have happened by chance.

MATHEMATICAL ODDS—1 in 100,000 = 1 × 10⁵

HIS GARMENTS WOULD BE PARTED AND LOTS CAST

PROPHECY by David 1000 B.C.

> They part my garments among them, and cast lots upon my vesture.
> —Psalm 22:18

PROPHECY FULFILLED about A.D. 30—The soldiers divided His outer garments, but could not decide on who would get His robe, so they cast lots for it. Several eyewitness accounts are recorded in the Bible:

> And they crucified him, and parted his garments, casting lots. . . .
> —Matthew 27:35

> And when they had crucified him, they parted his garments, casting lots upon them, what every man should take.
> —Mark 15:24

Then said Jesus, Father, forgive them; for they know not
what they do. And they parted his raiment, and cast lots.

—Luke 23:34

DISCUSSION OF ODDS—David foresaw this event a thousand years earlier, and it is a rather unusual way to divide
the spoils. Because most people in jails were poor, it was
the custom of the time for jailors to confiscate any valuables
of those who entered their jails. This was especially true
for those about to be executed, if the local officials hadn't
already directed that this property was to be turned over
to them or their government. I say one chance in 10 that it
could happen by chance.

MATHEMATICAL ODDS—1 in 10 = 1 × 10¹

HIS BONES WILL NOT BE BROKEN

PROPHECY by David 1000 B.C.

He keepeth all his bones: not one of them is broken.

—Psalm 34:20

PROPHECY FULFILLED about A.D. 30 AD—John 19:32–33
describes how the guards sought to end the crucifixion by
breaking the legs of the criminals:

Then came the soldiers, and brake the legs of the first,

and of the other which was crucified with him. But when they came to Jesus, and saw that he was dead already, they brake not his legs.

DISCUSSION OF ODDS—It was common practice to break the legs of crucifixion victims, because the victims used their legs to push up on the nails in their feet to relieve the pressure on their chests caused by hanging from the nails in their hands (or wrists). This pressure resulted in a slow suffocation. By breaking their legs, they hastened the victim's death, presumably so they could all go home sooner. Clearly they broke the legs of the thieves hanging next to Jesus, but not His. This concession to some degree of civility seems contrary to their previous actions considering the fact that they had spent almost the entire day physically and mentally abusing Him. I say there is one chance in 10,000 they avoided breaking His bones by accident.

MATHEMATICAL ODDS 1 in 10,000 = 1 × 10^4

HIS SIDE WOULD BE PIERCED

PROPHECY by Zechariah between 520–518 B.C.

And I will pour upon the house of David, and upon the inhabitants of Jerusalem, the spirit of grace and of supplications: and they shall look upon me whom they have pierced, and they shall mourn for him, as one mourneth

for his only son, and shall be in bitterness for him, as one
that is in bitterness for his firstborn.

—Zechariah 12:10

PROPHECY FULFILLED about A.D. 30—John 19:34 describes the event:

But one of the soldiers with a spear pierced his side, and
forthwith came there out blood and water.

Interestingly, Isaiah 53:5, written about 700 B.C., also describes this event:

But he was wounded for our transgressions, he was
bruised for our iniquities: the chastisement of our peace
was upon him; and with his stripes we are healed.

Also, Psalm 22:14 makes an allusion to a broken heart which
might have been caused by the spear:

I am poured out like water, and all my bones are out of
joint: my heart is like wax; it is melted in the midst of my
bowels.

DISCUSSION OF ODDS—Having beaten and crucified Christ,
with the cross standing erect, there was no chance that the
subject could possibly escape. In fact, death was clearly the
only outcome, and that was simply a matter of time. So what
would possess a soldier to pick up a spear and pierce the

side of Jesus? This is but another example of the continuing torture Christ endured at the hands of His captors. The odds are long but I suggest one chance in 100.

MATHEMATICAL ODDS—1 in 100 = 1 × 10²

HIS THIRST WILL BE QUENCHED WITH GALL AND VINEGAR

PROPHECY by David 1000 B.C.

> They gave me also gall for my meat; and in my thirst they gave me vinegar to drink.
>
> —Psalm 69:21

PROPHECY FULFILLED about A.D. 30—John 19:28–29 explains:

> After this, Jesus knowing that all things were now accomplished, that the scripture might be fulfilled, saith, I thirst. Now there was set a vessel full of vinegar: and they filled a spunge with vinegar, and put it upon hyssop, and put it to his mouth.

DISCUSSION OF ODDS—There is every reason to believe that someone nailed to a cross would become thirsty, and probably ask for something to drink. It is quite another thing to anticipate that a drink of vinegar would be offered.

Apparently, the soldiers intended to make fun of His situation, giving a dying man something repulsive to drink in His time of thirst. This incredible insult might have more easily been accomplished by offering brackish water or something foul, like rotten milk, or perhaps something even more contemptible. This was an era when, except for the few who drank wine, or goat's milk, most everyone drank water when they were thirsty. The odds of vinegar being offered are quite slim; I'd say one chance in 100,000.

MATHEMATICAL ODDS—1 in 100,000 = 1 × 10^5

GOD'S SERVANT WOULD BE BURIED IN A RICH MAN'S TOMB

PROPHECY by Isaiah about 712 B.C.

And he made his grave with the wicked and with the rich in his death; because he had done no violence, neither was any deceit in his mouth.

—Isaiah 53:9

PROPHECY FULFILLED about A.D. 30—Matthew 27:57–60 describes the burial of Jesus:

When the even was come, there came a rich man of Arimathaea, named Joseph, who also himself was Jesus' disciple: He went to Pilate, and begged the body of Jesus.

Then Pilate commanded the body to be delivered. And when Joseph had taken the body, he wrapped it in a clean linen cloth, And laid it in his own new tomb, which he had hewn out in the rock: and he rolled a great stone to the door of the sepulchre, and departed.

DISCUSSION OF ODDS—Families who could afford to purchased their own gravesites back then, as they do now. Jesus was poor by any monetary standard, and the likelihood of Him being buried in a rich man's tomb when He was not rich was virtually non-existent. By all accounts, He could have been buried in the very potters' field that the priests bought with the thirty pieces of silver Judas threw into the temple. I say there is one chance in 1,000,000 this happened by accident.

MATHEMATICAL ODDS—1 in 1,000,000 = 1 × 10⁶

THE MESSIAH (GOD OF OUR SALVATION) WILL STILL THE WINDS AND CALM THE WATERS

PROPHECY by David around 1,000 B.C.

By terrible things in righteousness wilt thou answer us, O God of our salvation; who art the confidence of all the ends of the earth, and of them that are afar off upon the sea: Which by his strength setteth fast the mountains;

being girded with power: Which stilleth the noise of the seas, the noise of their waves, and the tumult of the people.

—Psalm 65:5–7

Then they cry unto the LORD in their trouble, and he bringeth them out of their distresses. He maketh the storm a calm, so that the waves thereof are still.

—Psalm 107:28–29

PROPHECY FULFILLED about A.D. 30—Several accounts of Jesus calming the seas follow this event:

And when he was entered into a ship, his disciples followed him. And, behold, there arose a great tempest in the sea, insomuch that the ship was covered with the waves: but he was asleep. And his disciples came to him, and awoke him, saying, Lord, save us: we perish. And he saith unto them, Why are ye fearful, O ye of little faith? Then he arose, and rebuked the winds and the sea; and there was a great calm. But the men marvelled, saying, What manner of man is this, that even the winds and the sea obey him!

—Matthew 8:23–27

Mark 4:35–41 and Luke 7:22–25 offer slightly different accounts of the same story.

DISCUSSION OF ODDS—Modern man has experimented with ways to manage and affect the elements for decades.

One particular area of success is the process of "seeding" clouds to make it rain, but even that does not work all the time. Although any method that might work would have an enormous impact for agricultural purposes, there are also some military applications that would be employed, if the process were dependable. (In fact this was tried during the Vietnam War.) But making winds stop and calming seas is just not possible, even employing all of the tools of modern science. You can't do it, and I can't do it, and no man can make it happen. But I'll be generous and give it one chance in 1,000 that the seas were calmed by coincidence right at the time that Jesus asked the wind and the waves to be peaceful.

MATHEMATICAL ODDS—1 in 1,000 = 1 × 10³

THE SON WOULD BE THREE DAYS IN THE EARTH, LOST TO US ALL, BEFORE HE WOULD RISE AGAIN

PROPHECY by Moses around 1863 B.C.

Genesis 22 tells the story of Abraham's willingness to follow God's command and sacrifice his only son, Isaac. For three days the son was "lost" to him while he made preparations for the sacrifice, and then the angel of God stopped him. For those three days, the son was effectively lost to Abraham, before he was saved/found.

In a related prophecy which included the theme of being lost for three days, Jonah was in the belly of the whale for three days and three nights before being returned to the relative safety of dry land (Jonah 1:17–2:10).

PROPHECY FULFILLED about A.D. 30—Each account in Matthew, Mark, Luke, and John describes how the body of Jesus was taken from the cross and put in a tomb with a large stone across the entrance. A twenty-four–hour guard was placed on the tomb, and according to the tradition at the time, the guard was responsible for correctly doing his duty at the risk of his own life. It is reasonable to assume these guards carried out their responsibilities properly. After three days the two Marys came to see the tomb and discovered that the stone had been rolled away and the body of Jesus was gone.

DISCUSSION OF ODDS—This prophecy does not address the issue of whether or not Jesus rose from the dead. It only points out that the body would be in the ground for three days. Numerous texts document that it was three days from the point of the burial after the crucifixion until the stone was removed from the front of the tomb and the body was gone. (Math does not get much simpler. Three days in the grave would rule out a Friday burial and Sunday resurrection.) Christians believe that Jesus ascended into Heaven, but non-Christians argue that someone could have removed the body. Logic tells us that the local authorities would not have done this without also showing everyone that Jesus was simply dead, and dispelling any notion of His deity. His followers also would not have removed the body, believing that He would rise again through the power of God. And the guards would not have conspired to remove the body. Indeed, they probably lost their lives because the body was gone and they had been responsible for guarding it. The disappearance of the body after just three days by any means could not be an accident, but I'd call it one chance in 100.

MATHEMATICAL ODDS—1 in 100 = 1 × 10²

THE MESSIAH WILL OFFER HIMSELF AS A RANSON AND DIE FOR THE SINS OF ALL MEN

PROPHECY by Isaiah about 712 B.C.

> He shall see of the travail of his soul, and shall be satisfied: by his knowledge shall my righteous servant justify many; for he shall bear their iniquities.
> —Isaiah 53:11

PROPHECY FULFILLED about A.D. 30—Jesus describes how He would fulfill this prophecy by making a prophecy.

> Even as the Son of man came not to be ministered unto, but to minister, and to give his life a ransom for many.
> —Matthew 20:28

The essence of His message is that He accepted the sins of all mankind and died for all men who lived in the past, present, or future. But it is up to each person to accept the gift He offered.

DISCUSSION OF ODDS—The basic message of the New Testament is that Christ died for all our sins. It is perhaps difficult for non-Christians to accept this, but Isaiah knew seven hundred years before Christ was born that He would come and die for all of us. Due to the basic fact that this act was the fundamental mission of the Messiah, and to the level of doubt in the world, I would assign a very high probability of one chance in 10 that this happened by accident.

MATHEMATICAL ODDS—1 in 10 = 1 × 10¹

WHEN YOU TELL THE PEOPLE ABOUT GOD AND SALVATION, THEY WILL NOT BELIEVE IT

PROPHECY by Isaiah about 759 B.C.

And he said, Go, and tell this people, Hear ye indeed, but understand not; and see ye indeed, but perceive not.

—Isaiah 6:9

PROPHECY FULFILLED about A.D. 30

Therefore speak I to them in parables: because they seeing see not; and hearing they hear not, neither do they understand. And in them is fulfilled the prophecy of Esaias, which saith, By hearing ye shall hear, and shall not understand; and seeing ye shall see, and shall not perceive: For this people's heart is waxed gross, and their ears are dull of hearing, and their eyes they have closed; lest at any time they should see with their eyes, and hear with their ears, and should understand with their heart, and should be converted, and I should heal them. But blessed are your eyes, for they see: and your ears, for they hear. For verily I say unto you, That many prophets and righteous men have desired to see those things which ye see, and have not seen them; and to hear those things which ye hear, and have not heard them.

—Matthew 13:13–17

And he said, Unto you it is given to know the mysteries of the kingdom of God: but to others in parables; that seeing they might not see, and hearing they might not understand.

—Luke 8:10

DISCUSSION OF ODDS—Throughout life, one sometimes hears the refrain, "you can tell them and show them but they won't accept it." And there are quite a number of people that simply refuse to accept any message of salvation that requires them to alter their situation or their actions. It's possible that Isaiah got lucky with this one, so I assign it odds of one in 10.

MATHEMATICAL ODDS—1 in 10 = 1 × 10¹

THIS PROPHECY SUMS UP THE COMING OF THE MESSIAH

PROPHECY by Isaiah about 740 B.C.

> For unto us a child is born, unto us a son is given: and the government shall be upon his shoulder: and his name shall be called Wonderful, Counseller, The mighty God, The everlasting Father, The Prince of Peace. Of the increase of his government and peace there shall be no end, upon the throne of David, and upon his kingdom, to order it, and to establish it with judgment and with justice from henceforth even for ever. The zeal of the LORD of hosts will perform this.
>
> —Isaiah 9:6–7

PROPHECY FULFILLED about A.D. 30—The Gospels of Matthew, Mark, Luke, and John describe the entire story of how Jesus arrived on Earth, conducted His ministry, offended the local religious and government leaders, was tried, crucified, buried, and resurrected, and how He appeared to His disciples before ascending into Heaven. Jesus fulfills numerous prophecies made about the Messiah spoken of in the Old Testament and the Jewish holy books.

DISCUSSION OF ODDS—Isaiah was used by God to describe many details about the coming of the Messiah and how He would be a beacon for all mankind. It is certainly possible that he guessed well, as many Old Testament passages anticipate a Savior. He could easily have guessed at certain events that would eventually happen, but it is very unusual that he got so many details correct, and missed none. To be conservative, I'd give it one chance in 100 that this story was told then happened entirely by accident.

MATHEMATICAL ODDS—1 in 100 = 1 × 10²

God said in Isaiah 40:10–11:

> Behold, the Lord GOD will come with strong hand, and his arm shall rule for him: behold, his reward is with him, and his work before him. He shall feed his flock like a shepherd: he shall gather the lambs with his arm, and carry them in his bosom, and shall gently lead those that are with young.

He promised the world He would send a Messiah. Does it seem likely that He already has? Does Jesus Christ fulfill that promise? Should we wait around for someone else to come along and fulfill that role? Wouldn't that mean that the New Testament has no validity? Let no man deceive you. No one can decide these things for you. You must make up your own mind and hopefully the science of math will help you decide.

What Are the Odds?

The essence of mathematics is not to make simple things complicated, but to make complicated things simple.

—S. Gudder

WE HAVE EXAMINED FORTY PROPHECIES AND THE EVENTS AND EYEWITNESS ACCOUNTS THAT SHOW THEY WERE FULFILLED. Obviously, all these proceedings could have first been guessed at, and then happened individually by accident, but keep in mind we are faced with a much more unique and complicated prophecy. That is the fundamental message of the coming Messiah, that all these events happened to the same man, born centuries after the prophecies were made by a number of individuals who did not know each other and did not even live at the same time. And all the prophecies were fulfilled at about the same time in history. What are the odds that all of this happened by accident?

To find the odds of all the events happening, we need to multiply the odds of each event happening times each of the other events. Just like we did for the odds of a single person being struck by lightning and also winning the lottery. It is as simple as that.

Modern math helps us do this calculation easily. Remember the mathematician's use of the power of ten tool for manipulating very large numbers. We use this rather simple concept as a shorthand method. This permits us to multiply a series of large numbers by counting the number of zeros in each individual event, so that we do not have to write out long numbers including all these zeros and commas.

Each one of the forty prophecies has been assigned a conservative probability in terms of one chance in ten, one hundred, one thousand, ten thousand, etc. Using the shorthand math process described, I converted each one to one times ten to the tenth power simply by identifying the number of zeros. It is that easy. Note that this was already done for each prediction.

Using the power of ten, we can effortlessly calculate the combined probability of all the events happening to the same man as predicted hundreds of years earlier simply by multiplying the ones times the ones, which of course equals one, and then adding the total number of zeros. This shorthand method simply saves us from the tedious longhand process of multiplying ten times one hundred, then multiplying the result by one thousand, then multiplying again by ten thousand, and so on. The results are eye-opening, if not truly shocking.

THE COMBINED PROBABILITY OF ALL THESE FORTY EVENTS HAPPENING IS ONE TIMES TEN TO THE 136TH POWER (10^{136}). That's a 1 with 136 zeros! You might want to get out a piece of paper and try to write a 1 with 136 zeros on it,

just to get an idea of how large this number really is. Assuming you didn't do that (and even if you did), I can put the number in perspective for you.

Your next question might go something like this: It sounds like a very large number, but how large is it really? Well, a normal pinhead can hold about 5 million atoms. That could be written as 5×10^5. This number sounds not so big when written in the power of ten. Look at something larger. A drop of water consists of about 100 billion atoms. That would be 1×10^{11}, certainly a larger number, but not even remotely on the order of the odds of forty events happening by accident. Something larger might put our number in better perspective.

Take you personally as an example. How many atoms are there in you? Let's assume you are an average human and you weight about 155 pounds. A detailed analysis of all the hydrogen, oxygen, and carbon in you would show that you have about 7×10^{27} atoms in your body. You might say this as 7 billion, billion, billion atoms, but 7×10^{27} atoms is much easier to both say and write.

That is still not nearly as large a number as we got in our analysis of forty prophecies, so let's look at another larger example. Scientists have estimated the weight of the Earth, and from this we can calculate a rough approximation of the number of atoms it contains. Reliable estimates are that this planet we live on contains about 1×10^{50} atoms.

You might be thinking that this can't be correct, since

COL. STEPHEN M. BAUER

the exponent of fifty is almost twice the exponent of twenty-seven, giving the appearance that the number of atoms in the Earth is twice the number of atoms in an average sized human body. But of course you must remember that each time we add another zero to the exponent (ie: taking 10^{27} and making it 10^{28}), we are saying that the new number is ten times larger than the previous one. So the number of atoms in the Earth has twenty-three more zeros in it than the number of atoms in an average human.

Still, the number of atoms in the Earth is not nearly as large as the number calculated for the forty prophecies, so let's consider everything we can see, even using the Hubble space telescope. Estimates are that the observable universe, including all the planets, moons, and stars in the entire sky, contains approximately 1×10^{81} atoms. Now that is a large number. If you were to write this out, it would look like this:

1,000,000,000,000,000,000,000,000,000,000, 000,000,000,000,000,000,000,000,000,000, 000,000,000,000,000,000,000 atoms in the known and observable universe.

That is an astonishingly large number, but even a calculation of an estimate of all the atoms in our entire observable universe is a number considerably smaller than the odds of these forty prophecies coming to pass. That has to be a mighty sobering thought, especially for someone who does not believe in Jesus Christ as the Messiah.

While the odds of all these forty events coming to pass

and happening to the same man are extraordinarily low, this calculation does not even consider the additional odds of all these events happening at the same time. The Bible reports that at one point in time, some men were living for hundreds of years. For example, Methuselah died when he was 969 years old. We do not allow that kind of time to pass for these forty events to transpire, but we do not add more "chance" for the probability calculation of simultaneous fulfillment, even though that might be fully justified. Adjust your own thinking accordingly as to how all these events could happen at about the same time. To do that, you will have to add some amount of zeros you think is appropriate.

The preceding forty events cover only a few of the many dozens of prophecies in the Bible concerning the Messiah. And these prophecies about the Messiah only address an incredibly small portion of the total number of predictions made in the Bible. Think about those other prophecies we have not addressed. Some of them might be very easy to explain in terms of probability, while others are certainly more difficult.

If you arbitrarily assigned a one chance in ten to the remainder of the dozens of prophecies, that would add a number of additional zeros to the one chance in 10^{136} we have already estimated with just forty events. That would be a number so large it would probably have well over one hundred and fifty zeros after it. It is simply incomprehensible that such odds would happen by chance.

Here are just some of the many additional prophecies

COL. STEPHEN M. BAUER

about the coming Messiah that are not included in the above calculations. You can evaluate for yourself and assign your own odds that each one of these might have been predicted, and then come true completely by accident. Don't forget to at least mentally add the new zeros to the 10^{136} previously calculated for the forty prophecies.

PROPHECY: **He would commit Himself to God**—In Psalms 31:5, David wrote 1,000 B.C.:

> Into thine hand I commit my spirit: thou hast redeemed me, O LORD God of truth.

FULFILLED: Luke wrote about the time of Christ:

> And when Jesus had cried with a loud voice, he said, Father, into thy hands I commend my spirit: and having said thus, he gave up the ghost.
> —Luke 23:46

PROPHECY: **His friends would stand far away**—In Psalms 38:11 David wrote 1,000 B.C.:

> My lovers and my friends stand aloof from my sore; and my kinsmen stand afar off.

FULFILLED: Luke wrote about the time of Christ:

> And all his acquaintance, and the women that followed him from Galilee, stood afar off, beholding these things.
> —Luke 23:49

In this prophecy, the reference to "lovers" does not mean what it does today. These are His very close family members.

PROPHECY: The Messiah would be smitten by His captors—Micah wrote 700 B.C. in chapter 5, verse 1:

> Now gather thyself in troops, O daughter of troops: he hath laid siege against us: they shall smite the judge of Israel....

FULFILLED: Matthew wrote about the time of Christ in Matthew 26:67:

> Then did they spit in his face, and buffeted him; and others smote him with the palms of their hands,

PROPHECY: He would voluntarily die for us—In Psalm 40:6–8, David wrote 1,000 B.C.:

> Sacrifice and offering thou didst not desire; mine ears hast thou opened: burnt-offering and sin-offering hast thou not required. Then said I, Lo, I come: in the volume of the book it is written of me, I delight to do thy will, O my God: yea, thy law is within my heart.

FULFILLED: John wrote about the time of Christ in John 10:11,17–18:

> I am the good shepherd: the good shepherd giveth his life for the sheep.... Therefore doth my Father love me, because I lay down my life, that I might take it again. No

man taketh it from me, but I lay it down of myself. I have power to lay it down, and I have power to take it again. This commandment have I received of my Father.

PROPHECY: He would thirst—In Psalm 69:3,21 David wrote 1,000 B.C.:

I am weary of my crying: my throat is dried: mine eyes fail while I wait for my God. . . . They gave me also gall for my meat; and in my thirst they gave me vinegar to drink.

In Psalm 22:15, David wrote:

My strength is dried up like a potsherd; and my tongue cleaveth to my jaws; and thou hast brought me into the dust of death.

FULFILLED: In John 19:28, we read:

After this, Jesus knowing that all things were now accomplished, that the scripture might be fulfilled, saith, I thirst.

PROPHECY: Darkness would cover the land—Amos wrote 788 B.C. in chapter 8, verse 9:

And it shall come to pass in that day, saith the Lord GOD, that I will cause the sun to go down at noon, and I will darken the earth in the clear day.

FULFILLED: Matthew wrote about the time of Christ in Matthew 27:45:

Now from the sixth hour there was darkness over all the land unto the ninth hour.

You may consider this prophecy to simply be an amazing coincidence that a full eclipse of the sun occurred on this particular day and precisely at this hour. Consider that we have observed many solar eclipses in modern times and we know that an eclipse of the sun rarely lasts more than a few minutes, and never an hour, let alone three hours. This event could not have been an accident.

***PROPHECY:* He will ask God why He has forsaken Him—** In Psalm 22:1–5, David wrote 1,000 B.C.:

> My God, my God, why hast thou forsaken me? why art thou so far from helping me, and from the words of my roaring? O my God, I cry in the daytime, but thou hearest not; and in the night season, and am not silent. But thou art holy, O thou that inhabitest the praises of Israel. Our fathers trusted in thee: they trusted, and thou didst deliver them. They cried unto thee, and were delivered: they trusted in thee, and were not confounded.

FULFILLED: Matthew wrote about the time of Christ:

> And about the ninth hour Jesus cried with a loud voice, saying, Eli, Eli, lama sabachthani? that is to say, My God, my God, why hast thou forsaken me?
>
> —Matthew 27:46

***PROPHECY:* His appearance would make Him unrecognizable**—Isaiah wrote 700 B.C. in chapter 52, verse 14:

As many were astonied at thee; his visage was so marred more than any man, and his form more than the sons of men.

FULFILLED: Luke and John wrote about the time of Christ:

And it came to pass, that, while they communed together and reasoned, Jesus himself drew near, and went with them. But their eyes were holden that they should not know him.

—Luke 24:15–16

And when she had thus said, she turned herself back, and saw Jesus standing, and knew not that it was Jesus. Jesus saith unto her, Woman, why weepest thou? whom seekest thou? She, supposing him to be the gardener, saith unto him, Sir, if thou have borne him hence, tell me where thou hast laid him, and I will take him away. Jesus saith unto her, Mary. She turned herself, and saith unto him, Rabboni; which is to say, Master. Jesus saith unto her, Touch me not; for I am not yet ascended to my Father: but go to my brethren, and say unto them, I ascend unto my Father, and your Father; and to my God, and your God.

—John 20:14–17

But when the morning was now come, Jesus stood on the shore: but the disciples knew not that it was Jesus.

—John 21:4

This has to relate to the fact that the torture of Christ before

He was crucified included the tearing off of His facial hair, making Him unrecognizable later.

PROPHECY: He would commit His spirit to God at the end—In Psalm 31:5 David wrote 1,000 B.C.:

> Into thine hand I commit my spirit: thou hast redeemed me, O LORD God of truth.

FULFILLED: Luke wrote about the time of Christ:

> And when Jesus had cried with a loud voice, he said, Father, into thy hands I commend my spirit: and having said thus, he gave up the ghost.
>
> —Luke 23:46

PROPHECY: He is so great He can walk on water—Assume Elihu wrote Job around 1,650 B.C.:

> Then Job answered and said, I know it is so of a truth: but how should man be just with God? If he will contend with him, he cannot answer him one of a thousand. . . . Which alone spreadeth out the heavens, and treadeth upon the waves of the sea.
>
> —Job 9:1–3,8

FULFILLED: Matthew wrote about the time of Christ:

> And in the fourth watch of the night Jesus went unto them, walking on the sea. And when the disciples saw

him walking on the sea, they were troubled, saying, It is a spirit; and they cried out for fear.

—Matthew 14:25–26

PROPHECY: The Messiah will begin His ministry in the land of Zebulun and Naphtali—Isaiah wrote 740 B.C.:

Nevertheless the dimness shall not be such as was in her vexation, when at the first he lightly afflicted the land of Zebulun and the land of Naphtali, and afterward did more grievously afflict her by the way of the sea, beyond Jordan, in Galilee of the nations. The people that walked in darkness have seen a great light: they that dwell in the land of the shadow of death, upon them hath the light shined.

—Isaiah 9:1–2

FULFILLED: Matthew wrote about the time of Christ:

And leaving Nazareth, he came and dwelt in Capernaum, which is upon the sea coast, in the borders of Zabulon and Nephthalim: That it might be fulfilled which was spoken by Esaias the prophet, saying, The land of Zabulon, and the land of Nephthalim, by the way of the sea, beyond Jordan, Galilee of the Gentiles; The people which sat in darkness saw great light; and to them which sat in the region and shadow of death light is sprung up. From that time Jesus began to preach, and to say, Repent: for the kingdom of heaven is at hand.

—Matthew 4:13–17

PROPHECY: **A root of Jesse will attract the gentiles**—Jesse was the father of David, and the house of David was destined to rule over the house of Jacob (Israel) forever. We now know that Jesus Christ was also a descendent of the house of David through Mary's lineage. Isaiah wrote 700 B.C. :

> And in that day there shall be a root of Jesse, which shall stand for an ensign of the people; to it shall the Gentiles seek: and his rest shall be glorious.
>
> —Isaiah 11:10

FULFILLED: Paul wrote about the time of Christ:

> And again, Esaias saith, There shall be a root of Jesse, and he that shall rise to reign over the Gentiles; in him shall the Gentiles trust.
>
> —Romans 15:12

Many gentiles and a few Jews have come to trust and accept a root of Jesse (Jesus Christ). Perhaps you should be one of them.

PROPHECY: **A cornerstone would be placed in Zion**—That cornerstone would be Jesus Christ, the Messiah. Isaiah wrote 700 B.C.:

> Therefore thus saith the Lord GOD, Behold, I lay in Zion for a foundation a stone, a tried stone, a precious corner stone, a sure foundation: he that believeth shall not make haste.
>
> —Isaiah 28:16

FULFILLED: Paul wrote about the time of Christ:

> As it is written, Behold, I lay in Sion a stumblingstone and rock of offence: and whosoever believeth on him shall not be ashamed.
>
> —Romans 9:33

And Peter wrote about the time of Christ:

> Wherefore also it is contained in the scripture, Behold, I lay in Sion a chief corner stone, elect, precious: and he that believeth on him shall not be confounded. Unto you therefore which believe he is precious: but unto them which be disobedient, the stone which the builders disallowed, the same is made the head of the corner, And a stone of stumbling, and a rock of offence, even to them which stumble at the word, being disobedient: whereunto also they were appointed.
>
> —1 Peter 2:6–8

Reference to a "stumblingstone" is that the example Christ sets would be an impediment to all those who do not follow His guidance living on Earth and getting into Heaven to be with God, His Father.

PROPHECY: They would smite the shepherd and the sheep would be scattered—Zechariah wrote between 520–518 B.C.:

> Awake, O sword, against my shepherd, and against the man that is my fellow, saith the LORD of hosts: smite the

shepherd, and the sheep shall be scattered: and I will turn mine hand upon the little ones.

—Zechariah 13:7

FULFILLED: Matthew wrote about the time of Christ:

Then saith Jesus unto them, All ye shall be offended because of me this night: for it is written, I will smite the shepherd, and the sheep of the flock shall be scattered abroad. . . . But all this was done, that the scriptures of the prophets might be fulfilled. Then all the disciples forsook him, and fled.

—Matthew 26:31,56

Mark 14:27,50 offers an identical account of the words of Jesus and the actions of His disciples as they deserted Him for a while.

PROPHECY: **Elijah the prophet would come before the Lord comes**—Malachi wrote between 450–400 B.C.:

Behold, I will send you Elijah the prophet before the coming of the great and dreadful day of the Lord: And he shall turn the heart of the fathers to the children, and the heart of the children to their fathers, lest I come and smite the earth with a curse.

—Malachi 4:5–6

FULFILLED: Matthew wrote about the time of Christ:

> For all the prophets and the law prophesied until John.
> And if ye will receive it, this is Elias, which was for to
> come.
>
> —Matthew 11:13–14

> And his disciples asked him, saying, Why then say the
> scribes that Elias must first come? And Jesus answered
> and said unto them, Elias truly shall first come, and
> restore all things. But I say unto you, That Elias is come
> already, and they knew him not, but have done unto him
> whatsoever they listed. Likewise shall also the Son of
> man suffer of them. Then the disciples understood that
> he spake unto them of John the Baptist.
>
> —Matthew 17:10–13

Mark 9:11–13 and Luke 1:16–17 present similar descriptions of how John the Baptist represents Elijah and how he was treated.

My interpretation of the prophecy is that the "great day of the Lord" is the day He came to die for all our sins on the cross. The "dreadful" day will be the day He comes back to judge us all. Whether or not this is correct, the return of Elijah is clearly described as the ministry of John the Baptist.

PROPHECY: God told Abram that everyone on Earth will be blessed because of him

> And I will bless them that bless thee, and curse him that
> curseth thee: and in thee shall all families of the earth
> be blessed.
>
> —Genesis 12:3

FULFILLED: The four gospels tell the story of the arrival of Jesus Christ the Messiah, who died on the cross for the benefit of all men. That some choose not to accept His offer of salvation does not negate the fact that He made the offer by dying for each one of us, and we are all blessed with this opportunity.

Historical Events Documented

INCLUDING THE DOZENS OF PROPHECIES WE HAVE MEN-
TIONED, THERE ARE APPROXIMATELY TWO THOUSAND
PROPHECIES IN THE BIBLE, ABOUT THE MESSIAH, ISRAEL,
HISTORICAL EVENTS AND THE FUTURE OF THE WORLD. We
have examined how some of these two thousand prophecies
have already happened. But here are a few others that also
happened. Read the stories, think about the possibilities,
and assign your own estimate of the odds of these events
occurring by pure chance. Remember, the odds of all these
events being correctly predicted, and then coming to pass
are in addition to all the prophecies previously mentioned.

The Decree of Cyrus

Around 700 B.C., the prophet Isaiah foretold that a conqueror named Cyrus would allow the Israelites to return
to Jerusalem and rebuild its temple.

> That saith of Cyrus, He is my shepherd, and shall perform
> all my pleasure: even saying to Jerusalem, Thou shalt be
> built; and to the temple, Thy foundation shall be laid.
> — Isaiah 44:28

When this prophecy was made, Cyrus did not even exist and the temple in Jerusalem was standing and in full operation. It was more that one hundred years later, in 586 B.C., that Nebuchadnezzar, the Babylonian king, sacked Jerusalem, destroyed the temple, and scattered the Jews who were not killed.

About 539 B.C., the Babylonian Empire was itself conquered by the Persians. King Cyrus (who was born in 580 B.C., several generations after Isaiah lived) then issued a formal decree allowing the Jews to return to Jerusalem and rebuild the temple. This decree has been confirmed by archaeologists who found a stone cylinder that describes the major events of Cyrus' reign, including this decree.

How could Isaiah possibly have known centuries earlier that the Jews who were in Jerusalem would have to leave and therefore need to return someday?

How could Isaiah know that the temple which stood would be destroyed and need rebuilding?

And how could Isaiah possibly know that a man named Cyrus would be born, would be a conqueror, and would allow the Jews to both return to Jerusalem and rebuild their temple? It might even be pointed out that this all happened during a time when Jews were generally persecuted by almost everyone, but then there has seldom been a time in history when that was not the case. The exceptionally kind reaction of Cyrus to the needs of the Jewish people was completely contrary to established norms of the relations between the Jews and everyone else.

Even if Cyrus was a more common name than history

records show, it was not a common occurrence for Jewish people to be overrun and scattered into other lands. And the destruction of the temple in Jerusalem was all but unthinkable to the Jewish people.

The odds of all these events happening just as Isaiah predicted are truly astronomical, but archaeologists have confirmed that they did happen. The message that Isaiah gave to the world well in advance of the actual events had to come from some source of information with a detailed knowledge of the future, which was unavailable to mortal man then, and is still unavailable to man today (except for the prophecies in the Bible.)

The Fall of Tyre

Chapter twenty-six of the Book of Ezekiel, written in 586 B.C., describes the fall of the city of Tyre (Tyrus) on the mainland to Nebuchadnezzar. It goes on to describe a siege against the island fortress of Tyre (a half mile off the coast of the mainland) two hundred fifty-three years later. Ezekiel said the invaders would tear down the ruins of the mainland city and throw them into the sea.

History shows that Alexander the Great laid siege to the island fortress in 332 B.C., two and a half centuries after Ezekiel made his prediction. Alexander's army made sure that the ruins of the city were thrown into the sea, although fulfilling the prophecy was not their objective. The army very cleverly used the discarded stones and rubble from the destroyed city to build a causeway to the island to defeat the inhabitants, thus fulfilling a biblical prophecy made nearly two and a half centuries earlier.

It is hardly conceivable that this all happened by accident. Ezekiel must have had some divine guidance in making his predictions hundreds of years earlier because it is not possible that the proud and independent Alexander the Great was simply reading from a script and following "instructions."

Daniel Chronicles the Greek Empire and Alexander

The book of Daniel was written around 550 B.C.. Chapter eleven records the ancient history of Babylon and Greece from the time Darius the Mede became king of Babylon until well after Alexander the Great died and turned his empire over to his generals.

> Also I in the first year of Darius the Mede, even I, stood to confirm and to strengthen him. And now will I shew thee the truth. Behold, there shall stand up yet three kings in Persia; and the fourth shall be far richer than they all: and by his strength through his riches he shall stir up all against the realm of Grecia. And a mighty king shall stand up, that shall rule with great dominion, and do according to his will. And when he shall stand up, his kingdom shall be broken, and shall be divided toward the four winds of heaven; and not to his posterity, nor according to his dominion which he ruled: for his kingdom shall be plucked up, even for others beside those.
>
> —Daniel 11:1–4

The true identity of Darius the Mede is in some question, with several scholars suggesting his identity is attributed to several historical figures who were in Babylon at this time. The three kings of Persia were sons and a son-in-law of Cyrus the Great. Cambyses II and his brother Smerdis were followed by Darius I. Xerxes was the son of Darius who married one of the daughters of Cyrus. Xerxes led an army across the Hellespont to subjugate the Greek mainland.

The "mighty king" of verse three was Alexander the Great who at the age of twenty was made king when his father was assassinated. Alexander went on to become one of the most successful generals of all time, conquering both Persia and Egypt and much of the known world.

At the very young age of thirty-two, Alexander died under unusual circumstances. Some said he was poisoned and others thought he had malaria. His kingdom was quickly divided up by his four generals, they having been key players in its creation through their skillful military exploits in carrying out Alexander's orders. His children were either too young at the time, mentally incompetent, or not considered legitimate offspring, having been born of a concubine.

The net result of the breakup of Alexander the Great's empire produced four separate kingdoms. Egypt, Syria, Greece, and Asia Minor emerged under the leadership of those who succeeded Alexander's four generals, fulfilling the prophecy of Daniel in unique detail.

Daniel 11:5–19 also details the history (centuries in advance) of the Near East. Egypt became the kingdom of the south with a series of kings named Ptolemy. The kingdom of the north was Syria under Seleucus, who was succeeded by Antiochus I and II and Seleucus II. Scripture tells a complicated story of how they would interact (from alliances to treachery) in such detail that it defies logic to suggest that Daniel made a series of lucky guesses. The only real explanation is he had divine guidance.

> The hardest arithmetic to master is that which enables us to count our blessings.
>
> —Eric Hoffer

The Odds Increase

O NLY FORTY EVENTS SURROUNDING THE MESSIAH WERE USED TO DETERMINE A PROBABILITY OF ONE CHANCE IN TEN TO THE 136TH POWER THAT THIS SEQUENCE OF EVENTS ALL HAPPENED BY ACCIDENT TO THE SAME MAN. Have you taken issue with some of my estimates of the probabilities? I tried to be fairly conservative in my assignment of probabilities, but do you think some of these figures should be even more conservative? Rather than one chance in a million, should it be one chance in one hundred thousand? Simply reduce the number of zeros by one. Do you want to do that in several places? Be my guest. At the same time, you must consider that I might have been too conservative in other places. Is it possible that you want to add more zeros, making the odds even longer than I anticipated? That too is a personal choice.

Should the total odds be only ten to the 130th power, or even ten to the 120th power? Or should the odds be ten to the 140th power? (Don't forget to assign some extremely low probability to the other biblical prophecies about the Messiah, and assign some odds to the predictions that concerned the other prophecies.)

When you add them all up, the differences in opinion

THE MATH OF CHRIST

about a couple of these forty events are ultimately relatively minor considering both the increases and reductions you made. And this number does not include the probabilities that you assigned to the preceding examples of Bible prophecy that did not involve the Messiah directly.

So what do we do with this number? By now, you must have the opinion that ten to the 136th power really does sound like a large number. (Did you try writing it out on a piece of paper?) Consider how many seconds the universe has been in existence. Each year has 365.25 days, times twenty-four hours, times sixty minutes in an hour, times sixty seconds in a minute. That's almost 32 million seconds in a single year. I believe Ussher's timeline that the world is six thousand years old. But if you believe, as some scientists do, that the universe is 10 billion years old, then its age in seconds is 32 million seconds times 10 billion years. Using the power of ten shorthand, the answer is the universe is 3.2×10^{17}. We arrive at this by multiplying the numbers, and adding the zeros (3.2×10^7 [or 32 million seconds] × 10^{10} [or 10 billion years]).

At 15 billion years, the age of the universe in seconds is a mere 4.8×10^{17} ($32 \times 15 = 480$ or 4.8, plus all the zeros). Note that we just added 5 billion years to the theoretical age of the universe and it did not even add one more zero to the total age in number of seconds (just a quick example of how much one more zero means when using the power of ten). That is a huge number, but is considerably smaller than the total number of atoms in the universe at approximately 10 to the 81st power.

Clearly, the age of the universe in seconds and the number of atoms in the universe are dwarfed by the odds that these forty events concerning the life of the Messiah happened by chance. If you consider the many dozens of other prophecies concerning the coming of the Messiah, and even some of the many hundreds of other biblical prophecies, the odds become considerably larger. And the implications for every man, woman, and child on Earth become more dramatic.

> Mathematics is the supreme judge; from its decisions there is no appeal.
>
> —Tobias Dantzig

The Father of Probability Theory

WE ALREADY KNOW THAT SOMEONE CAN BUY A LOTTERY TICKET AND WIN A LARGE SUM OF MONEY WITH VERY LONG ODDS BECAUSE IT HAPPENS ONCE OR TWICE A YEAR AS REPORTED BY THE MEDIA. But does the concept of achieving something even despite very long odds, prove the existence of the Messiah spoken of in the Old Testament and the Jewish holy books? It would be instructive to know what the mathematics profession tells us about these very large odds. To evaluate that question, we need to consult the teachings of the man that both scientists and mathematicians refer to as the father of probability theory.

Born to a French Protestant minister, Dr. Emile Borel (1871–1956), became one of the world's foremost experts on game theory and mathematical probability. He is credited with formulating what scientists and mathematicians alike refer to as the "basic law of probability".

> **The basic law of probability states that the occurrence of any event in which the chances are beyond 10^{50} or one in one followed by fifty zeroes (10 to the 50th power), is *an event that we can state with certainty will never happen,* no matter how much time is allotted and no matter how many conceivable opportunities could exist for the event to take place.**

What this tells us is that it is mathematically impossible for these forty events to have happened by chance. Think about that: it is a simple but extraordinarily profound statement based on the extensive work of one of the world's most noted experts on mathematical probability.

> **These forty events could not have all happened to the same man by accident.**

Adding in the possibility that other prophecies about the Messiah or historical events such as those described above happened by chance, makes the mathematical odds even more preposterous. Read the prophecy of Genesis 49:10 which proclaims that God's salvation would reach the ends of the Earth. It might occur to you that missionaries travel the world trying to reach people in person. But with modern technology such as the radio, satellite and cable television, and the Internet, the message certainly has already reached the ends of the Earth. Whether or not people listen is another question altogether.

Consider that entire Psalm 22, written a thousand years before Christ, foreshadows many aspects of his crucifixion. Isaiah 61, written around seven hundred years before Christ, clearly describes the ministry He undertook centuries later. Assign some conservative probability that these events could happen by chance and then add the zeros to the one chance in ten to the 136th power. The odds are getting much longer that these events (happening all about the same time to a single man) were just an amazingly incredible coincidence.

Bible prophecy is God declaring things that are to come. God directed Isaiah to write:

Remember the former things of old: for I am God, and there is none else; I am God, and there is none like me, Declaring the end from the beginning, and from ancient times the things that are not yet done, saying, My counsel shall stand, and I will do all my pleasure.

—Isaiah 46:9–10

And in Isaiah 48:3 we read:

I have declared the former things from the beginning; and they went forth out of my mouth, and I shewed them; I did them suddenly, and they came to pass.

The Italian physicist, mathematician, astronomer, and philosopher Galileo Galilei (1564–1642) played a major role in the Scientific Revolution. He has been called the "father of modern observational astronomy," the "father of modern physics," and "the father of modern science." He is often quoted on a variety of subjects, usually having to do with thinking and knowledge. One of his more famous quotations is, "Mathematics is the language in which God has written the universe." Clearly, one of the greatest thinkers of all time ties math to science and both to God. Perhaps the math described here will also bring you closer to God.

The History of the Jewish Nation Prophesies the Coming of Christ

THE HISTORY OF ISRAEL IS UNUSUALLY PROPHETIC OF THE COMING OF CHRIST AS THE MESSIAH. It foretells of His birth, His life through His ministry, His death, and His resurrection. Here are just a few key aspects of this great story told through the history of His chosen people.

From Abram Will Spring a Great Nation

Even before the State of Israel existed, God has alerted us to the coming nation and the Messiah it will produce. In talking to Abram, God tells him in Genesis 12:2–3:

> And I will make of thee a great nation, and I will bless thee, and make thy name great; and thou shalt be a blessing: And I will bless them that bless thee, and curse him that curseth thee: and in thee shall all families of the earth be blessed.

Abram is assured that God has chosen him to be the father

of a great nation, which we now know is Israel. But God also says that every family of the Earth will be blessed by this nation. Clearly, this tells us that in some way, someone from this nation to be will be a salvation for every man on Earth. We now know that this salvation was brought to Earth by a Jewish carpenter, Jesus Christ the Messiah.

Christ has offered this salvation to everyone who accepts it, but that does not mean everyone gets it automatically. It is a gift that must be willingly received, or it is a gift that is rejected.

One other aspect of this prophetic statement is the warning that God will bless them that bless Abram's offspring, but He will also punish those who curse his seed. This passage should offer great encouragement to any nation or world leader that supports Israel today, and it has ominous implications for many who are anti-Semitic. The proof of this is not what world leaders, politicians, friends, neighbors, or the general public thinks, but what God thinks.

Abraham Asked to Sacrifice His "Only" Son

Genesis 16 tells us how Sarai (later to be renamed Sarah) was greatly concerned that she was old and had never borne her husband Abram (later to be renamed Abraham) children. When she had not conceived and was getting quite old, Sarai sent him her own Egyptian handmaiden, Hagar, to bear him a child, and when that event occurred, the son was called Ishmael.

Chapter 17 tells us that as the names of Abram and Sarai were changed by God, He also made a covenant with

Abraham that he would be the father of many nations, and that his wife, Sarah, would be the mother of many nations after she conceived him a second son at age ninety. This son would be named Isaac. God also promised a covenant for both sons that they would be blessed with many offspring and the seed of both of them would become great nations.

In Genesis 21, Sarah decides that Hagar and Ishmael must leave so that he would not be an heir like Isaac. Hagar took Ishmael, raised him, and found him an Egyptian wife, who bore him sons that biblical scholars point out were the forefathers of the Arab world.

With Isaac now as the "only" son, God instructs Abraham in Genesis 22:2:

> And he said, Take now thy son, thine only son Isaac, whom thou lovest, and get thee into the land of Moriah; and offer him there for a burnt-offering upon one of the mountains which I will tell thee of.

This is, of course, quite a shock to Abraham to be instructed to sacrifice his only son, especially considering that God had already made a covenant with him that he would be the father of many nations. But he trusted God to resolve the problem created by the death of his only son.

The son Isaac was effectively "lost" to Abraham for three days . . .

> Then on the third day Abraham lifted up his eyes, and saw the place afar off.
>
> —Genesis 22:4

... before God said to Abraham in Genesis 22:12:

> And he said, Lay not thine hand upon the lad, neither
> do thou any thing unto him: for now I know that thou
> fearest God, seeing thou hast not withheld thy son, thine
> only son from me.

It should also be pointed out that Abraham went to "the land
of Moriah," as God instructed him, to sacrifice his only son.
This area is where Solomon would later build his temple,
and also where Jesus Christ as an only Son would be sacrificed, several thousand years in the future.

While this story may not appear in a prophetic form of
someone saying what will happen in the future, it clearly
portends the sacrifice of God's only Son who then is lifted up
three days later to walk again among His friends and followers. Isaac would also live to bear Jacob, who was renamed
Israel and eventually became the father of the twelve tribes
and the entire Jewish nation.

A Bride for the Son

The nation of Israel still did not exist, and to get there, Isaac
must first marry, then have offspring. In that day and age,
many marriages were arranged by fathers. Genesis 24 tells
us how Abraham wanted to find his son a wife from among
his own people, and not from among those that lived in the
surrounding land he was in at the time (Canaan).

Abraham sent his servant to find his son a bride. The
entire process of looking for a bride for his son is prophetic

of God or the Holy Spirit seeking a bride for Christ. The bride was found for both. Rebekah became the bride of Isaac and the mother of Jacob, who was renamed Israel by God. The Christian church became the bride of Christ.

The Scattering of the Jews, and Their Return to Palestine

Moses (with later contributions from Isaiah, Jeremiah, Hosea, Zechariah, and Jesus) prophesied that Judea would be conquered twice, with the Jews carried off as slaves. In 606 B.C., the Babylonians ruled over the Jews for a period of seventy years. Moses said the next conqueror would take the captive Jews to Egypt, selling them into slavery.

Moses was accurate on both accounts. Furthermore, God's prophets said the Jews would stay scattered throughout the world for several generations, but without becoming absorbed by the other nations and that eventually, the Jews would return to their land. This prophecy was fulfilled in 1948 when the State of Israel announced its Declaration of Independence, re-establishing the Jewish nation (Deuteronomy 29; Isaiah 11; Jeremiah 25; Hosea 3; Zechariah 13; and Luke 21).

The Passover

The Passover, perhaps more than any other story of the Hebrew nation, depicts the deity of Jesus Christ. It is a major historical event that actually took place in Egypt while the Jewish nation was in bondage, and Moses was trying to free them. He had gone to Pharaoh and asked him to "Let my people go." You saw it in the movie, but those Hollywood writers got it from the greatest writer of them all, because it was actually written in Exodus 5:1 by Moses:

> And afterward Moses and Aaron went in, and told Pharaoh, Thus saith the Lord God of Israel, Let my people go, that they may hold a feast unto me in the wilderness.

But God had plans to use Pharaoh to demonstrate His power over the gods of Egypt. He made sure that Pharaoh's heart was hardened, and he was unwilling to release the Israelites. God proceeded to bring a series of plagues upon Egypt to convince the Pharaoh to release the Israelites, but also to demonstrate His own power.

The first nine plagues made Pharaoh very nervous. He agonized over their meaning and their impact on Egypt, but he did not give in. The tenth plague unleashed by God to convince a doubting Pharaoh was that the firstborn of all the families in Egypt would die.

All the Hebrews knew that the angel of death could be turned away from their door if they sacrificed a lamb "without blemish," and sprinkled its blood over the doorpost, then consumed its body (does this sound like part of the traditional Christian communion practice to you?). They did this and it saved the Hebrews from the loss of their firstborn, and placed all the resulting misery and death on the Egyptians, including the firstborn of Pharaoh (just like in the movie).

Seeing the death and destruction brought about by the God of Israel, the people of Moses were freed of their bondage in Egypt. Since then, they have celebrated this event as the Passover, when the Angel of Death passed over their doors because they had been sprinkled with the blood of the lamb "without blemish." The night this happened is commemorated and observed as the night of the 14th of Nisan, which is the end of the second week of the first month in the Jewish calendar.

The story of the Passover is a prophetic description of the death of Christ. Considered to be the only man ever born who was without sin (or blemish), as the Lamb of God He was crucified on the 14th of Nisan, according to Christian tradition. He rose again from the dead on the 17th of Nisan. The details of the death of Christ on the cross are in perfect harmony with and mirror the traditional Jewish version of the Passover.

As an interesting side note, there is no biblical reference for the secular fear of Friday the 13th, but there are some historians who believe that the Jewish evening of the 14th of Nisan (which began at six p.m. on the 13th) was in fact a Friday. That night, all of the firstborn of Egypt died, creating a terrible superstitious fear in the land, and this is what these historians believe gave rise to the notion that Friday the 13th is an unlucky day (especially if you are Egyptian). Today, the fear of Friday the 13th is also referred to as *triskaidekaphobia*.

Raising a Symbol on a Pole

There are numerous events in the history of Israel that foretell of the life and death of Christ. Another one is the story of the Israelites wandering in the wilderness for forty years. Frustrated after being homeless for so long, they complained about Moses and about the way God was treating them. To punish them, God sent fiery serpents which bit and killed many of them.

> And the LORD sent fiery serpents among the people, and they bit the people; and much people of Israel died.
>
> —Numbers 21:6

When the people finally repented, the Lord instructed Moses to raise a fiery serpent on a pole, for those who were bitten to look upon, that they would be healed. Moses did this with a brass serpent raised on a shaft. This is very specifically prophetic of Christ being raised on the cross to suffer for the sins of the world and thereby offer salvation for everyone in the world. Those that would place their faith in Him would also be saved. John 3:14-15 quotes Jesus as saying:

> And as Moses lifted up the serpent in the wilderness, even so must the Son of man be lifted up: That whosoever believeth in him should not perish, but have eternal life.

It should be noted that a double brass serpent on a rod has become the symbol of medical healing today, largely because the U.S. Army adopted it at the beginning of the twentieth century for the Medical Service Corps. Known as a *caduceus* or the wand of Hermes, it was originally (and erroneously) thought that this was a representation of healing. In fact, the rod of Asclepius (the god of medicine in old Greek mythology) with only one serpent on a pole would have been much more appropriate.

Ironically, Hermes was the Olympian god of travelers, business and commerce, and cunning thieves and liars, so the use of two serpents on a pole suggests something other than what the profession of medicine intended. Ultimately and indirectly, medicine adopted this emblem from the biblical story.

Daniel Is Cast Into the Lion's Den

Nebuchadnezzar elected to take a number of hostages back to Babylon after the kingdom of Judah was overrun. Daniel and three other young men of noble birth—Hananiah, Mishael, and Azariah—were among those taken to insure the cooperation on the conquered people. (Most people will not be aware that Daniel was given the new name Belteshazzar, but most everyone will recognize the names that the other three were given: Shadrach, Meshach and Abednego.)

Following several years of training, and after Daniel correctly interpreted a number of dreams for the king, he was elevated to a lofty position in the king's court. Later, his three companions refused to worship the golden idol offered by King Nebuchadnezzar and were thrown into a fiery furnace as punishment. The furnace was so hot that the men who threw them in were killed, but the three in the furnace were protected by an angel, and when the king looked into the furnace he saw four men, with the fourth looking like the Son of God. The king was so impressed that he called these three men out, praised them and their god, and promoted them in his government. See Daniel 3.

Jealous rivals to Daniel in the court succeeded in getting the next king to sign a decree making the king the only diety. Their hidden agenda was to make sure that no one could make petitions to any god other than the self-proclaimed king, and all such activity would be punished. They were certain that Daniel would not follow this law, and they were not disappointed. Daniel continued to pray to his God, and for this he was thrown into the lion's den and a stone was placed over the entrance. See Daniel 6.

God once again sent an angel to protect Daniel, and when the king discovered that Daniel was still alive when the stone was removed, and he had not been eaten by the lions, Daniel was returned to a position of power and authority in the king's court. The men who tried to defeat him were fed to the lions along with their entire families.

Daniel sealed in a den with lions is prophetic of Jesus Christ sealed in the rich man's tomb. Although Daniel never died, he was assumed to be dead as the lions could be counted on to kill and eat anyone they could get hold of. Christ, in His human form, was dead when He went into the tomb, but, like Daniel, He was alive when He came out, as He walked among His disciples for many days before ascending into Heaven.

> I used to love mathematics for its own sake, and I still do, because it allows for no hypocrisy and no vagueness....
> —Stendhal

THE MATH OF CHRIST

The Message for You

YOU MUST DECIDE FOR YOURSELF IF THIS WAS AN ACCIDENT OF TIME THAT ALL THESE FORTY EVENTS HAPPENED BY CHANCE. While considering this possibility you must be aware that all the rabbis of all the tribes of Judah for the past two thousand years have insisted that Jesus Christ is not the Messiah spoken of in the Old Testament and the Jewish holy books. (They are still waiting for Him to come.) Essentially, the rabbis are saying that these forty events (along with the other prophecies and events surrounding Jesus Christ) did, in fact, happen by accident.

You must decide for yourself if it is just possible that these forty events did happen as predicted by His holy book because a God who exists outside our time constraints knows the future. Did He then guide His prophets to tell us about the future? Is it even remotely conceivable that all these prophets just made a series of lucky guesses?

If you think He exists, shouldn't you study more closely what He said? If He has told us how to live with Him for eternity, shouldn't we be concerned enough to examine His message?

♦ **We are all sinners.** "For all have sinned, and come short of the glory of God" (Romans 3:23).

- **We can have eternal life through Jesus Christ.** "For the wages of sin is death; but the gift of God is eternal life through Jesus Christ our Lord" (Romans 6:23).
- **To do so, you must be born again.** "Jesus answered and said unto him, Verily, verily, I say unto thee, Except a man be born again, he cannot see the kingdom of God" (John 3:3).
- **Jesus Christ is the only way to Heaven.** "Jesus saith unto him, I am the way, the truth, and the life: no man cometh unto the Father, but by me" (John 14:6).
- **You must repent of your sins.** "I came not to call the righteous, but sinners to repentance" (Luke 5:32).
- **You must confess Jesus as your personal Lord and Savior, and believe He was raised from the dead.** "That if thou shalt confess with thy mouth the Lord Jesus, and shalt believe in thine heart that God hath raised him from the dead, thou shalt be saved. For with the heart man believeth unto righteousness; and with the mouth confession is made unto salvation. For the scripture saith, Whosoever believeth on him shall not be ashamed. For there is no difference between the Jew and the Greek: for the same Lord over all is rich unto all that call upon him. For whosoever shall call upon the name of the Lord shall be saved" (Romans 10:9–13).
- **Jesus waits at the door for you to open it.** "Behold, I stand at the door, and knock: if any man hear my voice, and open the door, I will come in to him, and will sup with him, and he with me. To him that overcometh will I grant

to sit with me in my throne, even as I also overcame, and am set down with my Father in his throne" (Revelation 3:20–21).

But you must open that door yourself. No one else can do it for you. If you think you can live somewhat like a Christian, and God will meet you halfway on Judgment Day, then you are likely in for a very rude awakening according to the Scriptures.

Trying to live a godly life and being nice to other people is a wonderful way to live, but it isn't going to get you into Heaven. Sitting in church does not make you a Christian, just like sitting in the garage does not make you a car.

And contrary to some interpretations of Christian doctrine, doing good deeds isn't going to get you into Heaven either.

> Knowing that a man is not justified by the works of the law, but by the faith of Jesus Christ, even we have believed in Jesus Christ, that we might be justified by the faith of Christ, and not by the works of the law: for by the works of the law shall no flesh be justified.
> —Galatians 2:16

> Not of works, lest any man should boast.
> —Ephesians 2:9

> Who hath saved us, and called us with an holy calling, not according to our works, but according to his own

purpose and grace, which was given us in Christ Jesus
before the world began.

—2 Timothy 1:9

If doing good works could get you into Heaven, then the
entire point of the sacrifice of Jesus Christ on the cross is
wasted. You might be tempted to think that He didn't really
have to die. And that we just need to do good works to spend
eternity with God. Clearly, the Bible tells us that works will
not get you into Heaven. Only the acceptance of the gift of
eternal life offered by God through His Son and the sacrifice
He made on the cross will do. Nothing else will get you there.

But don't misunderstand. This does not mean that you
should not do good works. Indeed, quite the opposite is the
case, and Scripture tells us why:

What doth it profit, my brethren, though a man say he
hath faith, and have not works? can faith save him? . . .
Even so faith, if it hath not works, is dead, being alone.
Yea, a man may say, Thou hast faith, and I have works:
shew me thy faith without thy works, and I will shew thee
my faith by my works. . . . But wilt thou know, O vain man,
that faith without works is dead? Was not Abraham our
father justified by works, when he had offered Isaac his
son upon the altar? Seest thou how faith wrought with his
works, and by works was faith made perfect? . . . Ye see
then how that by works a man is justified, and not by faith
only. Likewise also was not Rahab the harlot justified by
works, when she had received the messengers, and had

sent them out another way? For as the body without the
spirit is dead, so faith without works is dead also.
—James 2:14,17–18,20–22,24–26

Good works comes from faith in Christ. Once you have
placed your faith in Him, you will be inclined to do the good
works the Bible speaks of. If works aren't necessary to get
into Heaven, then what do they accomplish?

For the Son of man shall come in the glory of his Father
with his angels; and then he shall reward every man according to his works.
—Matthew 16:27

All good works will eventually be rewarded in Heaven. I
believe your works determine the crowns you will receive
when you arrive, so it is certainly appropriate to do good
works whenever you feel moved to and whenever you can,
but do not believe that these works are all that is necessary
to get you into Heaven.

It was Martin Luther who challenged the religious
leaders in Rome when he first pointed out in the sixteenth
century that the Bible says we are justified by faith and not
by works. Martin Luther relied on three specific passages:

But that no man is justified by the law in the sight of God,
it is evident: for, The just shall live by faith.
—Galatians 3:11

Behold, his soul which is lifted up is not upright in him:
but the just shall live by his faith.

—Habakkuk 2:4

For therein is the righteousness of God revealed from
faith to faith: as it is written, The just shall live by faith.

—Romans 1:17

Martin Luther's protest became the basis for the Protestant Reformation. While a number of churches emerged following this period of enlightenment, Lutherans offered the initial challenge to the Catholic Church doctrine, which essentially said that believers could get truth from the proper interpretation of the Bible rather than from the very words of the Bible. This interpretation would come from the Catholic Church leadership, and their understanding and analysis of the words of the Bible would govern man.

God Himself, in His own book, has made it perfectly clear that following the Law will not get you into Heaven; you must have faith. However you achieve that faith, you must ultimately have it. While Martin Luther's publication of his discovery created the Protestant movement, it also encouraged learned peoples everywhere to study what the Bible itself says. Careful evaluation of what man says about the Bible's message has consistently identified flaws in some interpretations.

You can overcome the adversities of life on this Earth and spend eternity with God the Father, but this is a decision that only you can make for yourself. No one else can do this for you. Your family and friends while you are alive, and the ones you leave behind after you die, cannot pray you into Heaven. Also, they cannot buy your way into Heaven, regardless of how much money they have or how much they give to any church or charitable cause. You must choose before you die to seek and accept God on His terms, and not on some formula or system devised by man. Since it is very unlikely that you will know when you are going to die, perhaps you should think about getting right with God now.

> The laws of nature are but the mathematical thoughts of God.
>
> —Euclid

The Message Authenticated

JUST HOW ACCURATE IS THE MESSAGE OFFERED BY GOD IN THE BIBLE? In Isaiah 42:8–9, He tells us that He has made things foretold come true already, and He will prophesy other events to confirm His deity:

> I am the LORD: that is my name: and my glory will I not give to another, neither my praise to graven images. Behold, the former things are come to pass, and new things do I declare: before they spring forth I tell you of them.

Prophecy in the Bible has a real and specific purpose. Certainly, it was intended to confirm that God is real, but it also demonstrates quite clearly that He exists outside our universe of space and time.

We live in a world where time marches forward. You can never go back, regardless of how appealing it might be to redo some action or take something back that was said in haste. If this were possible, divorce court would be nearly empty, and there would be no lottery. We would all be buying last night's winning lottery ticket, meaning the prize might be split millions of ways, making the payoff meaningless. Everyone would win, so no one would bother to play.

Being outside the rigors of our time domain, God has already seen the future. He freely moves forward or backward in time. He already knows everything that will happen, and that is why it was so simple for Him to inform us through the words of His prophets of what will happen in a book written thousands of years ago.

God tells us what the future will hold in His book, the Bible. He guided specific prophets to write what the future will be, just so He could demonstrate His omnipotent power, and so you could accept His authority over the universe which He created. Then you might be led to accept Him, and join Him in eternity. It is, has been, and always will be your own personal choice to either accept or reject His offer of eternal life. But how do we know it is really an authentic message from God?

If you have never served in the military, certainly you have seen movies that show important instructions from higher headquarters sent to subordinates that require confirmation. This is usually done by identifying the sender by sight or sound of their voice.

Written instructions, however, must also be authenticated. Simple documents can be verified as accurate by recognizing and accepting an ordinary signature or a common letterhead. More important messages such as something classified or a verbal communication over a wire or wireless system must undergo a more thorough process of confirming their authenticity. This is done through security tables of authenticating codes or physical key cards used in encryption devices.

Prophecy in the Bible is another way of God authenticating that the message of the Bible for you, the reader and believer, is divinely inspired. He actually tells you through His prophets what will happen, centuries before it does. Then when it happens, you should carefully evaluate the fact that you were alerted well in advance by an omnipotent being.

Consider the very simple, modern technology of Caller ID on your phone. It may not confirm that the information passed to you is accurate, but it certainly can tell you where it came from. Primarily because of new tools like Caller ID, crank calls sending taxis or pizza to someone who did not request them are, for the most part, a thing of the past.

Isn't the message received in a communication even more significant than the medium used to send it? The value of an honest check is always worth more than the paper it was printed on. If the message comes centuries ahead, but proves to be true, does that make it something we can easily ignore? Shouldn't we attach more credibility to a message that predicts certain events that couldn't just "happen by accident," but they do in fact happen? Wouldn't that mean the sender was truly awesome? Don't you wish you knew someone that could tell you the future? You can make Him your best friend and He will tell you your future for eternity.

Science in the Bible

God does not play dice with the universe.

—Albert Einstein

A NOTHER TECHNIQUE GOD USES IN THE BIBLE TO AUTHEN-
TICATE HIS MESSAGE IS TO REVEAL SCIENTIFIC FACTS,
LONG BEFORE MAN DISCOVERS THEM.

The World Is Round

For example, would you believe the Bible describes the
world as being round? Seven hundred years before Christ,
Isaiah wrote:

> It is he that sitteth upon the circle of the earth, and the
> inhabitants thereof are as grasshoppers....
>
> —Isaiah 40:22

The word translated here as "circle" is the Hebrew word
chuwg. It can also be interpreted as "compass" or "circuit."
Clearly, it describes God sitting on a world which is rounded,
spherical, or domed, and not something that is level or flat.

About thirty years after Christ was crucified, Luke
wrote:

> I tell you, in that night there shall be two men in one bed; the one shall be taken, and the other shall be left. Two women shall be grinding together; the one shall be taken, and the other left. Two men shall be in the field; the one shall be taken, and the other left.
>
> —Luke 17:34–36

Read it again with the following understanding: What Luke is describing is a round world, where some men are asleep at night, at the same time it is morning in another place and women are grinding grain for the day's meals, and in a third place it is the middle of the day where other men are working on a farm. The fundamental message that everyone should be ready at all times of the day or night coincidentally also describes a spherical world. Although it may not have been the point of the passage, this is clearly a description of a round Earth with the sun at different positions in the sky.

More than fourteen hundred years later, Columbus was sailing the Atlantic with crews in three different ships about to mutiny because as experienced sailors, they were absolutely certain that their ships were about to sail off a flat Earth. Certainly, there were many well-educated people who suspected that the Earth was round well before 1492, but no one had proved it until Columbus completed his voyage successfully. Isaiah and Luke both knew it though, more than a millennia before modern man could confirm it.

The Earth Floats in Space

The book of Job, written by an unknown author (many be-

lieve it was Moses, but the words suggest Elihu) describes
the Earth floating in space.

> He stretcheth out the north over the empty place, and
> hangeth the earth upon nothing.
>
> —Job 26:7

We know for certain that Job was written sometime before
the fifth century B.C. because Ezekiel mentioned Job in chapter 14, verse 14. Some scholars believe that Job was actually
the very first book of the Bible ever written. Moses might
have been the author, but Elihu is also sometimes credited
with writing the book. Whoever wrote it, they could not
know that the Earth was a free-floating piece of real estate
in space. Only a divine being could have led the author of
Job to make such a statement.

Blood Is Essential to Life

Approximately fourteen hundred years before Christ, Moses
wrote in Leviticus 17:11:

> For the life of the flesh is in the blood . . .

Do you find it amazing that even as recently as the birth
of the United States, men of "modern" medicine were still
bleeding people to make them well from various diseases
and maladies? The father of our nation, George Washington,
might very well have died from the bleeding he received
the morning before his death. Unaware of what was really

wrong with the retired president, Washington's medical advisors opened a vein and allowed his life-giving blood to flow out of him, undoubtedly imperiling his overall chances of survival.

It was sometime in the 1800s when men practicing medicine realized that humans needed all the blood they had to sustain their lives. Blood is necessary to transport oxygen throughout the body, as well as carrying waste away from cells. Also, blood helps regulate body temperature at the same time it is providing nourishment.

Had men of science and medicine read and heeded the Bible, they would have known for centuries how important blood is to life. Now, blood is commonly added to people in distress through transfusions, which of course does much more for their chances of survival and recovery than bleeding ever did.

Mental Health Influences Physical Health

In the ninth century before Christ, Solomon wrote in Proverbs 17:22:

> A merry heart doeth good like a medicine: but a broken spirit drieth the bones.

In the last few decades we have learned from many scientific sources that a person's attitude and mental disposition can greatly influence their physical health. A hearty laugh releases endorphins that enhance our natural healing ability and mask pain.

Conversely, depression has a serious negative impact on our physical well being. We now know that any detriment to our mental health has a corresponding harmful effect on our physical well being.

And all this was explained by Solomon centuries before Christ was born. George Washington would have been better served if they had brought in a comedian rather than the medical doctors he saw just before he died.

The Best Day for Circumcision

You might be aware that Hebrews were told that they must be circumcised to fulfill a covenant with God. You may not be aware that they were given a specific time that this should happen. Genesis 17:12 says:

> And he that is eight days old shall be circumcised among you. . . .

It has been a practice for most Jewish families to perform this act on the eighth day after birth specifically because Scripture demands it. Would you believe that modern science has now discovered a reason for doing this surgical procedure specifically on the eighth day after birth?

Prothrombin is a glycoprotein essential to the human body in the blood-clotting mechanism. It is produced in the liver, generally beginning around day five or six in the life of a newborn.

Scientists do not know what causes this medical condition, but Dr. Armand J. Quick discovered that prothrombin is at its highest level on the eighth day, and begins to decline on the ninth. The eighth day is therefore the optimal day to perform a surgical procedure which clearly causes bleeding like circumcision. The body would certainly benefit if it had an increased ability to clot the blood when a circumcision was performed.

Isn't it amazing that the discovery of prothrombin in the early 1900s revealed that what Moses wrote more than three thousand years earlier had a real scientific basis? If the medical community didn't know this until recently, then Moses sure could not have known it except by the intervention of an omnipotent being.

Rotate the Crops

When Moses wrote Leviticus around 1490 B.C. he clearly knew quite a bit about agriculture.

> And the LORD spake unto Moses in mount Sinai, saying, Speak unto the children of Israel, and say unto them, When ye come into the land which I give you, then shall the land keep a sabbath unto the LORD. Six years thou shalt sow thy field, and six years thou shalt prune thy vineyard, and gather in the fruit thereof; But in the seventh year shall be a sabbath of rest unto the land, a sabbath for the LORD: thou shalt neither sow thy field, nor prune thy vineyard.
>
> —Leviticus 25:1–4

Crop rotation has become one of the most important aspects

of modern farming. Not only does it give the land an opportunity to rejuvenate itself, but it increases crop yields and improves the lot of the farmer. Different crops both use and leave behind different chemicals, and letting a field rest for a season, growing nothing in particular, benefits all crops. And Moses knew this more than fourteen hundred years before Christ was born.

The Stars in the Sky Cannot Be Numbered

When Moses wrote Genesis 1,445 years before Christ was born, he made it clear that there were countless stars in the sky.

> That in blessing I will bless thee, and in multiplying I will multiply thy seed as the stars of the heaven, and as the sand which is upon the sea shore; and thy seed shall possess the gate of his enemies.
>
> —Genesis 22:17

The concept that there are a very large number of stars in the heavens was repeated by Jeremiah six hundred years before Christ.

> As the host of heaven cannot be numbered, neither the sand of the sea measured: so will I multiply the seed of David my servant, and the Levites that minister unto me.
>
> —Jeremiah 33:22

How does this relate to modern science? When these words were written, the only tool available to man to count the number of stars was the human eye. We know now that the human eye can distinguish only about twenty-five hundred stars in the sky. And that is on a good, clear night, without the interference of ambient city light, smoke or haze in the air, or modern pollutants. And it would be necessary to travel around the globe to see all these stars since when one is in the northern hemisphere, there are many stars that can only be seen from the southern hemisphere, and vice versa. We can assume with a great degree of certainty that neither Moses nor Jeremiah traveled this far to gauge the number of stars in the sky.

It was Galileo who first used a telescope in A.D. 1610 to identify many additional heavenly bodies such as the moons of Jupiter and numerous additional stars that had never been seen with the naked eye. His discoveries created a need for better instruments to study the heavens. More modern scientific devices were developed including the Hubble space telescope, which was launched by NASA in 1990 with Marine Colonel Charlie Bolden as the pilot.

Arguably the ultimate astronomical instrument available to man today, Hubble confirms that there are many billions and billions of stars in the sky, something neither Moses nor Jeremiah could have known without God's help. Each additional mission of NASA to improve the capability of Hubble merely confirms that we still do not know how many stars are in the sky. Ironically, on a clear night, we can not only see several thousand stars, but we can also see the Hubble space telescope pass overhead if we know where to look.

It is apparent to all that God did just what He said he would do, but in the prophecy He revealed His knowledge of science to us. Understanding the magnitude of that disclosure should help us conclude that there is a God and He is truly omnipotent.

Is this gift of prophecy unique to the Bible? You cannot find another sacred religious text that prophesies a coming Savior for all people of the world. As told in John 3:16–17, Jesus' purpose was to atone for all the sins of mankind:

> For God so loved the world, that he gave his only begotten Son, that whosoever believeth in him should not perish, but have everlasting life. For God sent not his Son into the world to condemn the world; but that the world through him might be saved.

All the sins of mankind includes all the sins man had committed up to the time of the crucifixion, as well as all the sins all men will commit until the end of the world as we know it.

Here is a humbling exercise. Think about the possibility that every sin you commit is part of the reason Christ suffered on the cross. The Jews may have been the instrument God used to save us through Christ's horrible death, but each of us bears personal responsibility for it whether we accept Him or not. Don't think I am being critical of the Jewish people. I thank them profusely for their part in my opportunity to attain salvation. If it weren't for the Jewish people and their role in presenting a Savior for the world we live in, God would have had to designate some other group as His chosen people. They fulfilled an absolutely essential role in the salvation of mankind.

There are dozens of people in the Bible who were prophets. Several books of the Old Testament are named after prophets: Isaiah, Jeremiah, Ezekiel, Daniel, Hosea, Joel, Amos, Obadiah, Jonah, Micah, Nahum, Habakkuk, Zephaniah, Haggai, Zechariah, and Malachi. Other prophets include Moses, King David, and Jesus Christ. All of these men were Hebrews.

If you are able to read Jewish scriptures (The Torah, The Prophets, and The Writings, which make up the Tenach or the Jewish Bible) you will see an elaborate description of many dozens of prophecies about the coming Messiah. They paint a very clear picture of who the Meshiach (Anointed One or Messiah) will be and what He will do when He comes to the nation of Israel. In Hebrew the name Jesus is Yeshua, meaning "God with us." Christ means "one who saves." The Greek word for messiah is "Christ" which is where we got the modern name for the Son of God through translations.

These prophets for the most part lived generations and centuries apart, dispelling any notion that they could have collaborated with each other in what they would say. More-over, they not only made their predictions independently, but they all made them well in advance of the future events they foretold. For the most part, every prophecy relates to a different aspect of the life and death and resurrection of Jesus Christ.

Were these prophets good at guessing future events, or unbelievably lucky, or inspired by God? Consider what God has to say:

All scripture is given by inspiration of God, and is profitable for doctrine, for reproof, for correction, for instruction in righteousness.

—2 Timothy 3:16

Knowing this first, that no prophecy of the scripture is of any private interpretation. For the prophecy came not in old time by the will of man: but holy men of God spake as they were moved by the Holy Ghost.

—2 Peter 1:20–21

All of these prophets must have been guided by an all-knowing all-powerful being to have accurately foretold the future. Mathematically, there is simply no room to believe that all these events were first predicted and then came to pass by accident.

Future Events in Bible Prophecy

THE BIBLE IS FULL OF PROPHECY, BUT THE BOOK OF REV-
ELATION IS PARTICULARLY NOTED FOR ITS VAST DESCRIP-
TION OF WHAT IS COLLECTIVELY KNOWN AS "THE END TIMES."
The Apostle John who also wrote the Gospel and the three
epistles which bear his name was exiled to Patmos, a Greek
island in the Aegean Sea off the coast of Turkey. The Roman government was intensely persecuting the Church
and the followers of Jesus because the Emperor Domitian
had proclaimed himself a god, and no one should worship
any other god.

John continued to preach the Word of God and greatly
disturbed the emperor and his court of followers, resulting
in John's banishment. John received this (book of) Revelation about Jesus Christ from God the Father while he was on
Patmos. Just as Genesis tells us about the beginning of time,
Revelation describes the end times. You should consider this
an indication that the Bible as it was written and exalted by
the Church for centuries, is actually a complete document, in
that it describes both a beginning and an end. No additions
were expected, desired, necessary, or appropriate.

The book of Revelation begins with a short account of

the author. A special blessing is promised to anyone who reads or hears the prophecies of this book and also keeps them. The book (and the Bible) end with a direct warning which I will cover later.

There are seven letters written by Christ and directed to seven specific churches of Asia Minor, which is modern-day Turkey. These were not at all the biggest or the most important churches of the time. In fact they were quite small congregations, but the message contained applies to all churches, both then and now, that fit one of the seven descriptions.

It has been suggested that these seven churches represent the history of the Christian Church beginning with Ephesus which might represent the age of the Apostles. Smyrna could describe the persecution of the Church following Christ's crucifixion.

Descriptions of Pergamos and Thyatira would be the recovery of the Church and the rise of papacy. Sardis would be the Reformation, leading to Philadelphia which exemplifies the missionary advances of the Church. And lastly, the description of the church of Laodicea illustrates the current times where so many people are falling away from Christ.

The book of Revelation goes on to explain seven seals, seven trumpets, seven signs, seven plagues, seven dooms, and seven new things. The book in its totality promises a complete understanding of the fate that awaits every human who ever lived, and how the end of life here on Earth is just the beginning of eternity. Whether you spend eternity with God or with Satan is entirely up to you.

The Last Days

This know also, that in the last days perilous times shall come. For men shall be lovers of their own selves, covetous, boasters, proud, blasphemers, disobedient to parents, unthankful, unholy, Without natural affection, trucebreakers, false accusers, incontinent, fierce, despisers of those that are good, Traitors, heady, high-minded, lovers of pleasures more than lovers of God; Having a form of godliness, but denying the power thereof: from such turn away. For of this sort are they which creep into houses, and lead captive silly women laden with sins, led away with divers lusts, Ever learning, and never able to come to the knowledge of the truth. Now as Jannes and Jambres withstood Moses, so do these also resist the truth: men of corrupt minds, reprobate concerning the faith. But they shall proceed no further: for their folly shall be manifest unto all men, as theirs also was. But thou hast fully known my doctrine, manner of life, purpose, faith, longsuffering, charity, patience, Persecutions, afflictions, which came unto me at Antioch, at Iconium, at Lystra; what persecutions I endured: but out of them all the Lord delivered me. Yea, and all that will live godly in Christ Jesus shall suffer persecution. But evil men and seducers shall wax worse and worse, deceiving, and being deceived. But continue thou in the things which thou hast learned and hast been assured of, knowing of whom thou hast learned them.

—2 Timothy 3:1–14

Does this description of the last days sound suspiciously like the world we live in today? Do you see the actions of friends, neighbors, relatives, and strangers, or perhaps even yourself in this scripture? I think this narrative very closely describes the attitude of man today. Consider what God told Daniel in 539 B.C.:

> But thou, O Daniel, shut up the words, and seal the book, even to the time of the end: many shall run to and fro, and knowledge shall be increased.
>
> —Daniel 12:4

Unquestionably, knowledge has increased substantially since Christ's crucifixion, and knowledge has increased dramatically in the past century. Using this newfound knowledge and filled with personal conceit, many people exhibit all of the worst traits known to history. And I'm not just referring to politicians or Hollywood celebrities. Radio, television, newspapers, magazines, and everyday conversation are filled with examples of man acting just like God said he would. And we can only hope we as individuals are ready for Him, when He comes.

The Second Coming of Christ

The arrival of Christ here on Earth again will come as a complete surprise to everyone: Luke wrote:

> And as it was in the days of Noe, so shall it be also in the days of the Son of man. They did eat, they drank, they

married wives, they were given in marriage, until the day that Noe entered into the ark, and the flood came, and destroyed them all. Likewise also as it was in the days of Lot; they did eat, they drank, they bought, they sold, they planted, they builded; But the same day that Lot went out of Sodom it rained fire and brimstone from heaven, and destroyed them all. Even thus shall it be in the day when the Son of man is revealed. In that day, he which shall be upon the housetop, and his stuff in the house, let him not come down to take it away: and he that is in the field, let him likewise not return back. Remember Lot's wife. Whosoever shall seek to save his life shall lose it; and whosoever shall lose his life shall preserve it. I tell you, in that night there shall be two men in one bed; the one shall be taken, and the other shall be left. Two women shall be grinding together; the one shall be taken, and the other left. Two men shall be in the field; the one shall be taken, and the other left.

—Luke 17:26–36

This passage describes the surprise people will feel when Christ comes again to Earth to gather all the brothers and sisters in Christ. It demonstrates how people around the globe will be in various stages of daily activity at the precise moment of the second coming of Christ. It refers to the actual return of Christ to Earth to preside over the last judgment of the living and the dead and to establish the Kingdom of God on Earth.

Many Christians refer to this time as the Rapture. The

word is not used in the Bible, but comes from the Greek word *harpazo,* which is translated as "caught up" in 1 Thessalonians 4:13–17:

> But I would not have you to be ignorant, brethren, concerning them which are asleep, that ye sorrow not, even as others which have no hope. For if we believe that Jesus died and rose again, even so them also which sleep in Jesus will God bring with him. For this we say unto you by the word of the Lord, that we which are alive and remain unto the coming of the Lord shall not prevent them which are asleep. For the Lord himself shall descend from heaven with a shout, with the voice of the archangel, and with the trump of God: and the dead in Christ shall rise first: Then we which are alive and remain shall be caught up together with them in the clouds, to meet the Lord in the air: and so shall we ever be with the Lord.

Christ will come back to Earth at the same time that the souls of those who have died in Christ and those who are living in Christ will rise into the air and proceed to Heaven with Him. This will also be a prelude to the establishment of Christ as the ruler of the Earth for a reign of one thousand years.

The Rapture is expected to happen at about the time of what is referred to as the Great Tribulation, which is the name given to the seventieth week of Daniel. In this account, a week is a term used to actually represent seven years. Daniel 9:24–27 describes these seventy weeks (or four hundred ninety years):

Seventy weeks are determined upon thy people and upon thy holy city, to finish the transgression, and to make an end of sins, and to make reconciliation for iniquity, and to bring in everlasting righteousness, and to seal up the vision and prophecy, and to anoint the most Holy. Know therefore and understand, that from the going forth of the commandment to restore and to build Jerusalem unto the Messiah the Prince shall be seven weeks, and threescore and two weeks: the street shall be built again, and the wall, even in troublous times. And after threescore and two weeks shall Messiah be cut off, but not for himself: and the people of the prince that shall come shall destroy the city and the sanctuary; and the end thereof shall be with a flood, and unto the end of the war desolations are determined. And he shall confirm the covenant with many for one week: and in the midst of the week he shall cause the sacrifice and the oblation to cease, and for the overspreading of abominations he shall make it desolate, even until the consummation, and that determined shall be poured upon the desolate.

Verses 24–26 describe the first sixty-nine weeks, while verse 27 describes the seventieth week, or the last seven years. Three views emerge from this: the first being that the Rapture will happen at the beginning of the last week, the second believing that the Rapture will come in the middle, or after three and a half years, and the last being that the Rapture will come after the week (seven-year period) is ended.

No one knows when this will happen, not even Jesus Christ Himself. Only God the Father knows. Matthew 24:36–44 describes an account of the words of Jesus (similar to Luke 17:26–36) as follows:

> But of that day and hour knoweth no man, no, not the angels of heaven, but my Father only. But as the days of Noe were, so shall also the coming of the Son of man be. For as in the days that were before the flood they were eating and drinking, marrying and giving in marriage, until the day that Noe entered into the ark, And knew not until the flood came, and took them all away; so shall also the coming of the Son of man be. Then shall two be in the field; the one shall be taken, and the other left. Two women shall be grinding at the mill; the one shall be taken, and the other left. Watch therefore: for ye know not what hour your Lord doth come. But know this, that if the goodman of the house had known in what watch the thief would come, he would have watched, and would not have suffered his house to be broken up. Therefore be ye also ready: for in such an hour as ye think not the Son of man cometh.

Not only can no one know when this day will come, just like the world did not know that a flood was coming when Noah entered the ark, but God warns us to be ready for His return at all times, just like the world should have been ready for a flood.

> But the day of the Lord will come as a thief in the night; in
> the which the heavens shall pass away with a great noise,
> and the elements shall melt with fervent heat, the earth
> also and the works that are therein shall be burned up.
>
> —2 Peter 3:10

Noah heeded God's warning, both saving himself, and offering the same opportunity to his wife and three sons. Will you heed God's warning?

The Christian Ministry of 144,000 Jews

For the past two thousand years, the Christian and Jewish religions have disagreed on whether or not the Messiah has already come to Earth in the form of Jesus Christ. And among Christian discussion groups, this controversy logically gives rise to what will become of God's "chosen people" if they do not accept Him. We should all be aware that there will be 144,000 Jews who are sealed as His own servants by God Himself in the last days:

> And I saw another angel ascending from the east, having
> the seal of the living God: and he cried with a loud voice
> to the four angels, to whom it was given to hurt the earth
> and the sea, Saying, Hurt not the earth, neither the sea,
> nor the trees, till we have sealed the servants of our God
> in their foreheads. And I heard the number of them which
> were sealed: and there were sealed an hundred and forty
> and four thousand of all the tribes of the children of
> Israel. Of the tribe of Juda were sealed twelve thousand.
> Of the tribe of Reuben were sealed twelve thousand. Of

the tribe of Gad were sealed twelve thousand. Of the tribe of Aser were sealed twelve thousand. Of the tribe of Nepthalim were sealed twelve thousand. Of the tribe of Manasses were sealed twelve thousand. Of the tribe of Simeon were sealed twelve thousand. Of the tribe of Levi were sealed twelve thousand. Of the tribe of Issachar were sealed twelve thousand. Of the tribe of Zabulon were sealed twelve thousand. Of the tribe of Joseph were sealed twelve thousand. Of the tribe of Benjamin were sealed twelve thousand.

—Revelation 7:2–8

The scripture makes it very clear that these 144,000 Jews will be servants of Christ. Literally, that means they will go out among the remainder of the Jews (and perhaps to gentiles as well) preaching the gospel of Christ the Messiah, and offering salvation through Him to the non-believers who do not yet accept Him. Note that the 144,000 are designated to come equally from each of the twelve tribes. This is probably to insure that the message Christ offers is available equally to all the Jews.

It is anyone's guess as to how many Jews will accept Christ after hearing from these tens of thousands of Jewish servants of God.

Several millennia have passed since the time that God gave his instructions to the descendents of Abraham, Isaac, and Jacob. They have functioned all this time under not just the well-known Ten Commandments, but also hundreds and hundreds of other laws, rules, practices, customs, and traditions.

From this it is fair to assume that the objective is to attempt to follow every guideline strictly. Picking and choosing the laws one will observe does not sound like a very constructive way to get into Heaven. Logically, we might conclude that it would be necessary to successfully observe every last one of these many obligations, or fail from a religious standpoint.

This highlights the fundamental message of the Christian faith, with Jesus Christ doing all the work for us by dying on the cross for the sins of all men. As we have seen in previous passages, this is something we cannot do for ourselves. We all must recognize His grace: God giving us something we do not deserve. And we must accept His mercy: God not giving us something we do deserve.

I personally believe that the Jews were first designated as God's chosen people to confirm their place under God's wing. In addition to wise and fair laws that serve as a witness to other nations, they were given so many obligations to observe that it would be apparent to all that no man could ever be successful at doing all of this on his own. Their trying and failing to complete all of these various religious requirements might be a message in itself that there has to be another and better way to get to Heaven.

Of course we now know that way is through the acceptance of Jesus Christ as a personal savior. And from Romans 11 (above), we also know that God has not forgotten his chosen people. They will be saved if they eventually come to believe in Jesus Christ.

This is another reminder that there has only been one man who ever lived on Earth that was perfect, and that man was Jesus Christ, the Son of God. Despite what some religious leaders tell you, no man has been or can be elevated to that status.

The Twelve Tribes of Israel

We have just seen how Revelation 7 describes the 144,000 Jews who are sealed in their foreheads as servants of Christ in the latter days. It should be noted that these twelve tribes are first identified as the twelve sons of Jacob (who was renamed Israel by God) in Genesis 29–30. In order of birth, they are:

1. Reuben (Genesis 29:32)
2. Simon (Genesis 29:33)
3. Levi (Genesis 29:34)
4. Judah (Genesis 29:35)
5. Dan (Genesis 30:5)
6. Naphtali (Genesis 30:7)
7. Gad (Genesis 30:10)
8. Asher (Genesis 30:12)
9. Issachar (Genesis 30:17)
10. Zebulun (Genesis 30:19)
11. Joseph (Genesis 30:23)
12. Benjamin (Genesis 35:18)

If you compare this list of sons with lists of the twelve tribes in various parts of the Bible, you will sometimes see different tribes listed. Just looking at Revelation 7:5–8, you will see that the tribe of Dan is not there. In its place is the tribe of Manasseh.

In Genesis 48, Jacob (Israel) blessed the two son's of Joseph, who were born in Egypt. These grandsons of Jacob, Manasseh and Ephraim, are sometimes substituted for Joseph in various lists of tribes.

In Revelation, Joseph is listed and Dan is omitted, God preferring to use Manasseh, the firstborn of Joseph. This is a rather deliberate slight to Dan, and there may be an explanation in Genesis 49:16–17:

> Dan shall judge his people, as one of the tribes of Israel.
> Dan shall be a serpent by the way, an adder in the path, that biteth the horse heels, so that his rider shall fall backward.

Just before he died, Jacob gave his final words of prophecy to his twelve sons, telling each about their futures and how he felt they and their offspring would fare. He singled out Dan, essentially saying that he (and his offspring) would be a significant problem for his brothers and their descendents. The fact that Dan was left off the list in Revelation 7 gives rise to the speculation among many students of the Bible that the Antichrist might well come from the tribe of Dan.

Jacob's final words to his sons also produced a special blessing for Joseph. He had been sold into slavery by his jealous brothers, but then rose to a very high position of authority in Egypt, and saved his family from starvation, along with the Pharaoh and all the people of Egypt.

Jacob had thought that he would never see Joseph again, and when he did he was overjoyed. In a major departure from the historical practice of the time of giving every firstborn male a double portion for his inheritance, Jacob conferred this honor on Joseph. Notice in the order of birth that Joseph was the eleventh son, not the first or even the last. And when God needed a replacement for the tribe of Dan in Revelation 7, he kept Joseph, and then included Joseph's firstborn son, Manasseh.

This obviously elevates Joseph above his brothers, but it particularly impacts Reuben, his firstborn son. When the Israelites conquer the land that God has designated for them, it is divided up among the various tribes. Joseph is not awarded a single portion, but rather Ephraim and Manasseh are each given a portion, which essentially gives Joseph two portions. Jacob (Israel) knew well in advance that this would happen because he was an instrument of God.

The Antichrist Comes

The following verses describe troubled times and the general mood of man being inclined away from God, and how this "void" is filled by the Antichrist.

Let no man deceive you by any means: for that day shall not come, except there come a falling away first, and that man of sin be revealed, the son of perdition; Who opposeth and exalteth himself above all that is called

God, or that is worshipped; so that he as God sitteth in the temple of God, shewing himself that he is God.

—2 Thessalonians 2:3–4

Once again, the term Antichrist is given to the being that comes to Earth to oppose Christ. He exalts himself above God, performing any act that might turn people from Christ, performing miracles to deceive believers, and generally causing any possible evil on Earth.

We are warned in several verses about the Antichrist and the spirit he embodies:

Little children, it is the last time: and as ye have heard that antichrist shall come, even now are there many antichrists; whereby we know that it is the last time.... Who is a liar but he that denieth that Jesus is the Christ? He is antichrist, that denieth the Father and the Son.

—1 John 2:18,22

And every spirit that confesseth not that Jesus Christ is come in the flesh is not of God: and this is that spirit of antichrist, whereof ye have heard that it should come; and even now already is it in the world.

—1 John 4:3

For many deceivers are entered into the world, who confess not that Jesus Christ is come in the flesh. This is a deceiver and an antichrist.

—2 John 1:7

The book of Revelation describes many despicable acts performed by the Antichrist, who actually goes by many names in the Bible, and in every case is an agent of Satan. We have just seen that in 2 Thessalonians 2:3 the Antichrist is referred to as the ***man of sin*** and ***the son of perdition.*** He is also known in the New Testament as:

- **That Wicked**—"And then shall that Wicked be revealed, whom the Lord shall consume with the spirit of his mouth, and shall destroy with the brightness of his coming" (2 Thessalonians 2:8).
- **The Angel of the Bottomless Pit**—"And they had a king over them, which is the angel of the bottomless pit, whose name in the Hebrew tongue is Abaddon, but in the Greek tongue hath his name Apollyon" (Revelation 9:11).
- **The Beast**—"And when they shall have finished their testimony, the beast that ascendeth out of the bottomless pit shall make war against them, and shall overcome them, and kill them" (Revelation 11:7).

Interestingly, the Old Testament also refers to the Antichrist in several places:

- **The Little Horn**—"I considered the horns, and, behold, there came up among them another little horn, before whom there were three of the first horns plucked up by the roots: and, behold, in this horn were eyes like the eyes of man, and a mouth speaking great things" (Daniel 7:8).
- **King of Fierce Countenance**—"And in the latter time of

their kingdom, when the transgressors are come to the full, a king of fierce countenance, and understanding dark sentences, shall stand up" (Daniel 8:23).

- **The Prince That Shall Come**—"And after threescore and two weeks shall Messiah be cut off, but not for himself: and the people of the prince that shall come shall destroy the city and the sanctuary . . ." (Daniel 9:26).

- **A Vile Person**—"And in his estate shall stand up a vile person, to whom they shall not give the honour of the kingdom: but he shall come in peaceably, and obtain the kingdom by flatteries" (Daniel 11:21).

- **The Idol Shepherd**—"Woe to the idol shepherd that leaveth the flock! the sword shall be upon his arm, and upon his right eye: his arm shall be clean dried up, and his right eye shall be utterly darkened" (Zechariah 11:17).

The Antichrist is the most significant agent of Satan here on Earth. He does the bidding of the fallen angel, trying to tempt man to follow a false path to eternity by following the devil rather than God the Father and His Son, Jesus Christ. He is a smooth talking, very charismatic person who wants to gather as many men and women away from the true path to eternity in Heaven as possible. And rest assured that he will be at least partly successful. But it would be to your advantage to anticipate this, especially if the Antichrist appears during your lifetime and offers something that sounds good to you. Be on your guard and reject anything that is not of God. Otherwise, you may spend eternity in the lake of fire with the Antichrist and Satan.

The Battle of Armageddon

The Antichrist, through one of his various names, will be a participant in many deceits against man in general and Israel in particular. Ultimately, he leads a number of armies against Christ at the battle of Armageddon where he is finally defeated.

There is only one reference in the Bible to Armageddon, found in Revelation 16:16:

> And he gathered them together into a place called in the Hebrew tongue Armageddon.

The word actually comes from the Hebrew *Har-Megido* which means "mountain of Megiddo." This is the site of the final struggle between good and evil, between Christ and Satan in the form of the Antichrist. When the Antichrist is defeated, he is thrown into the pit of fire along with Satan.

> And the beast was taken, and with him the false prophet that wrought miracles before him, with which he deceived them that had received the mark of the beast, and them that worshipped his image. These both were cast alive into a lake of fire burning with brimstone. And the remnant were slain with the sword of him that sat upon the horse, which sword proceeded out of his mouth: and all the fowls were filled with their flesh.
>
> —Revelation 19:20–21

The Antichrist and Satan in the Bottomless Pit

Satan is then bound for a thousand years and cast into the bottomless pit.

> And I saw an angel come down from heaven, having the key of the bottomless pit and a great chain in his hand. And he laid hold on the dragon, that old serpent, which is the Devil, and Satan, and bound him a thousand years, And cast him into the bottomless pit, and shut him up, and set a seal upon him, that he should deceive the nations no more, till the thousand years should be fulfilled: and after that he must be loosed a little season.
>
> —Revelation 20:1–3

The Millennium

Christ will then assume His position in Jerusalem as the King, fulfilling the prophecy that a descendent of the line of David (which we learned came through Mary's genealogy) is once again on the throne. In fact He rules the world for a thousand years, heralding the start of the millennial reign.

Revelation 20 goes on to explain how Satan is released after the thousand years to try and deceive the nations of the Earth. He is once again defeated by God sending fire upon them, and Satan and his followers are thrown into the lake of fire for eternity.

God's Final Judgment

The Great White Throne of God appears with Him sitting in judgment of everyone who has ever lived. Each person will then answer to God for everything they have ever done, and they will be rewarded according to these works. Those who have accepted Christ as their Lord and Savior will have their names written in the Book of Life. Everyone else will be thrown into the lake of fire for eternity and suffer everlasting torment. This is called the second death. This means you have died once here on Earth, and you effectively die again in front of God. Those who believe in the Bible refer to this sequence of life-changing events as being born only once here on Earth (by natural childbirth), meaning you must eventually die twice, even though the second "death" is really suffering eternal punishment.

The alternative is to be born twice: once naturally, and again in Christ. This would then mean you were born twice, and will only die once when you leave this Earth (skipping the second death in the lake of fire), and spending eternity in Heaven with God and Jesus Christ, the Messiah.

These events in this chapter (collectively referred to as **the end times**) have not come to pass because they are clearly labeled as future events. Many people reject the possibility that they will actually happen, largely because they don't believe in Christ in the first place.

We have already seen how many predictions and prophecies made by the messengers of God and given to us in His Word, the Bible, have already come to pass. And of course we have seen that the odds of these events happening by accident are too long to even be considered as chance occurrences.

Therefore, it stands to reason that there is simply no basis to conclude that the many hundreds of prophecies in the Bible related to future times will not also come to pass. You should now be in a position to accept this as a very sure thing. And of course you reject it at your own peril.

Choose Sides

GIVEN THAT THE BIBLE IS SUCH A RELIABLE DOCUMENT, YOU DECIDE IF JESUS CHRIST WAS THE MESSIAH SPOKEN OF IN THE HEBREW AND CHRISTIAN TEXTS, AND IF HE CAME TO SAVE YOU. And then you must decide which world view you accept. There are only two choices: did we evolve from a lightning strike on some random protoplasm cells in the mud of some swamp following some cataclysmic "big bang" event that created the universe, or were we created by an omnipotent being?

1) Is the human race simply the result of a series of cosmic and biological accidents?

Could our ancestors have really crawled out of the ocean or the muck of a swamp and started breathing air with lungs after using only gills to survive? Did we evolve from apes? If so, why didn't the apes evolve too?

Could something as complex as a human eye (let alone a human body) have developed from a blob of protoplasm struck by lightning? (Even Charles Darwin expressed concerns about the validity of his theory of evolution with regards to the development of the exceptionally complex human eye.) Would a series of mutations over centuries or millennia produce a continuous line of higher order animals, when mutants in today's animal world routinely die off early without reproducing?

Why have we never found a credible "missing link"? Probably because the "link" does not exist. Frauds of "links" exist, but no one has really produced a true link in the so-called evolution of the species.

Some scientists have gone so far as to identify fossils which they believe are the predecessors of modern-day animals. They cite geologic studies which prove that these animals existed millions of years ago, and evolved into some animal living today. This analysis indicates that all animals from prehistoric times evolved, but they have some difficulty explaining something like a coelacanth. Thought to be extinct for millions of years, several have been recently caught and surprisingly they look exactly like the prehistoric version locked in a fossil. You can go and see one for yourself in the Los Angeles Museum of Natural History.

"What about dinosaurs?" you ask. Genesis 1 describes clearly that they were made along with many other creatures and man on the sixth day of creation. In chapter 40 of Job, we hear more about dinosaurs than almost any other animal mentioned in the Bible.

Here is a much less scientific opinion, but nevertheless an interesting perspective on the chance that life evolved by itself on just one planet in the universe. Dr. Carl Sagan, the famous American astronomer and astrochemist from Cornell University who led the Search for Extra-Terrestrial Intelligence, wrote more than a dozen books and hundreds of scientific papers.

In his book *The Cosmic Connection*, Sagan offered his opinion as to the odds of evolution just happening. Sagan said that the probability of man evolving from a lower life form was one chance in ten to the 2 billionth power. That would be a ten with 2 billion zeros after it. This is a very, very, very large number indeed. (And we thought that 1×10^{136} was a rather large number.) Clearly, he was making an educated guess, but his vast experience in studying the stars and the universe gives a lot of credibility to the only real alternative to evolution.

2) Or are we the result of a purposeful design?

If we didn't evolve, then is our existence part of a plan by an omnipotent being who not only designed us, but designed the world we live in? You must believe one or the other. There is no other alternative.

If our world was designed for us, how would we know it? The **anthropic principle** states that the entire universe was designed to make life here on Earth as we know it possible. There are dozens of characteristics of our universe that would cause life to cease to exist on our planet if they were to be slightly altered.

If the axial tilt of the Earth were slightly changed, the differences in surface temperatures (both highs and lows) would make life impossible.

If the axial tilt did not change but the Earth took much longer than twenty-four hours to rotate completely, daily high and nightly low temperature differences would be too great to support life. If the rotation period were much shorter, surface winds would be too strong for life.

If the rate of lightning discharge in the atmosphere was much greater, there would be too much destruction from fire. If it were appreciably less, there would not be enough nitrogen fixation in the soil for life to continue.

If the Earth's rotation took it just a few degrees closer to the sun, the surface temperatures would be higher than the boiling point of water, precluding any life from sustaining itself. And if it we were just a few degrees farther from the sun in our rotation, the levels of carbon dioxide would be so high that man would not be able to breathe.

There are numerous other examples of how finely tuned our existence is here on Earth. Scientists are continually trying to explain how unique our world is to be able to support carbon-based life as it does. Most refuse to accept the possibility that our world was designed specifically for us by an omnipotent being.

Which world view do you accept? It is simply not possible for both evolution and creation to explain our existence. Everything we do stems from our belief in one or the other of these points of view. Those who advocate that both views can be true are simply in denial about making a decision, one way or the other. Straddling the fence may work well for politicians, but there is only one vote that counts in Heaven, and you don't get to make it.

If you believe we are the result of randomness, then you should not be at all surprised when you see others acting without any sense of decency or moral responsibility. On the other hand, if you accept that we are the product of a Designer, then perhaps you want to find out more about His plans for you.

"Jesus loves you" is what the children's song says and what every real Christian declares. At one point in your life your parents might have also told you that "Santa loves you" too. The difference is that Jesus Christ is real and His love knows no end, as long as you are willing to accept Him.

What Should You Do Next?

GOD MAKES MANY CLAIMS IN THE BIBLE, BUT HE ALSO AS-
SURES US OF ITS INERRANCY:

> All scripture is given by inspiration of God, and is profit-
> able for doctrine, for reproof, for correction, for instruc-
> tion in righteousness.
>
> —2 Timothy 3:16

Everything in the Bible comes from God Himself. None of
the stories or prophecies is the creation of the men who are
credited with writing them down. They only wrote what God
led them to write. And modern interpretations of what God
said should be very suspect to you. Believe what the Bible
actually says, and consider very carefully the men who tell
you "what it really means".

Have you decided to study the Bible more? If so, that
will be to your everlasting benefit, but beware of what you
study and who teaches you. Matthew 24:4–5 explain:

> And Jesus answered and said unto them, Take heed that

no man deceive you. For many shall come in my name, saying, I am Christ; and shall deceive many.

Start with the absolute undeniable premise that the only infallible man who ever lived on Earth was Jesus Christ. All other men (and women) are flawed sinners and subject to make mistakes. This includes every Bible teacher, every pastor, every minister, every man who calls himself a Christian leader, every author (that would include me), and every "man of the cloth," regardless of what cloth he represents. Despite what some people say, every man on Earth is a sinner and is imperfect, so don't be misled by the words of men—rely entirely on the Word of God.

You should read the Bible itself for spiritual guidance. Interpret it for yourself and ask other men whose opinions you respect what they think, but make sure they can support their positions with quotes from the Bible. Do not blindly accept what they say as "gospel." Make sure what they say is in the Gospel. Acts 17:11 explains that the Bereans did it right:

These were more noble than those in Thessalonica, in that they received the word with all readiness of mind, and searched the scriptures daily, whether those things were so.

Perhaps the most important step you can take when studying the Bible is to pray for guidance and understanding each time before you start. Prayer is most assuredly the most important tool you can use to discover how the Bible speaks to each one of us, no matter who we are, where we live, what language we speak, or why we feel compelled to understand it.

Occasionally, you will hear voices say that it is not appropriate to take the Bible literally. I disagree for the fundamental reason that to say that God did not mean exactly what He said in His book is to suggest that He made a mistake. That is simply not possible. The omnipotent being that created this universe, this Earth, everything in it, and mankind in all his enormous complexity, could not possibly err in sending us a message through His book.

Which Bible to use is another subject that could deserve an entire book by itself, and several have been written on the subject. In general, I recommend that you not use any modern translation. There are more than five hundred different versions of the Bible today, most of them written in the past one hundred fifty years. The authors of these newer versions usually have an agenda and interpret God's Word in such a way as to support that cause. They will twist the meaning of God's Word to satisfy their own objectives, relegating God's objectives to the back seat, if indeed they get presented at all.

One blatant example is a modern Bible version which says that God is a woman. Nothing in history other than the modern feminist movement suggests that this is the case, yet some poorly informed people assert that God is a woman simply because they have read this Bible version, or they just want to believe it. Other modern versions make social statements in their interpretations of the Bible. Don't be taken in by a modern man's version of God's ancient Word.

Personally, I use the King James Version, as you have seen throughout this text. Other versions that are almost the same are the Tyndale, or Geneva Bibles. They all come from manuscripts referred to as the Textus Receptus. This version was first published in the early part of the sixteenth century, and generally referred to translations of the Greek version of the New Testament. Together with translations of the Hebrew Old Testament, they form what I believe is the most accurate translation of God's Word in English. And they come without a political spin attached, as so many modern versions possess. Additionally, these older versions have a greater than 90 percent correlation with the many thousands of historical writings found by archaeologists.

Remember, God's Word cannot be copyrighted. If you happen to see a Tyndale, Geneva, or King James Version of the Bible that claims a copyright, it is probably due to notations or footnotes added or the technique in presenting the words, such as highlighting in red the words of Jesus. The text of the KJV cannot be copyrighted, which is one of the reasons that it is normally much less expensive to purchase in a book store.

You cannot be misled by God's personal message. But you can easily be misled by men twisting His message to support their interpretation of the Bible. And you should not rely on a single verse for doctrinal guidance. Everything said in the Bible is important, but the more important something is, the more often it is repeated. Reading and studying the

Bible thoroughly will insure that you hear and receive God's message for you. Second Timothy 4:3 warns:

> For the time will come when they will not endure sound doctrine; but after their own lusts shall they heap to themselves teachers, having itching ears.

Your best teacher is yourself reading the Bible after you have prayed for guidance. Understand that these sixty-six books written by forty different authors over a period of several thousand years are a detailed message from the Creator of the universe and everything in it. The Bible is designed to be your guidebook to living for eternity with God.

I mentioned earlier that there was a warning at the end of Revelation and the end of the Bible. Consider God's final admonition in Revelation 22:18-20:

> For I testify unto every man that heareth the words of the prophecy of this book, If any man shall add unto these things, God shall add unto him the plagues that are written in this book: And if any man shall take away from the words of the book of this prophecy, God shall take away his part out of the book of life, and out of the holy city, and from the things which are written in this book. He which testifieth these things saith, Surely I come quickly. Amen. Even so, come, Lord Jesus.